IMAGES
of America

# LONG ISLAND'S
# GOLD COAST

**HAYS AT KEEWAYDIN.** Hays Browning is pictured in front of his parents' summerhouse, Keewaydin, at Sands Point, shortly after its completion in late 1912. His father, John Scott Browning, owned Browning King & Co., a clothier based out of New York. The family's main residence was 270 Park Avenue in New York City. Keewaydin was one of several houses said to serve as a model for Daisy's fictional house in F. Scott Fitzgerald's *The Great Gatsby*. (BFA.)

**ON THE COVER: BEACON TOWERS, 1917–1918.** Said to be the inspiration for Jay Gatsby's home in F. Scott Fitzgerald's *The Great Gatsby*, Beacon Towers was built by the widow Alva Vanderbilt Belmont in 1917–1918. Alva paid $12,000 per acre for the tip of Sands Point, which bordered the lighthouse. Designed by Hunt & Hunt, the house was sold in 1927 to William Randolph Hearst and was occupied by his wife, Millicent, until 1942. It was razed in 1947. (VAN.)

IMAGES
*of America*

# LONG ISLAND'S
# GOLD COAST

Paul J. Mateyunas

ARCADIA
PUBLISHING

Published by Arcadia Publishing
Charleston, South Carolina

Library of Congress Control Number: 2011938170

For all general information, please contact Arcadia Publishing:
Telephone 843-853-2070
Fax 843-853-0044
E-mail sales@arcadiapublishing.com
For customer service and orders:
Toll-Free 1-888-313-2665

Visit us on the Internet at www.arcadiapublishing.com

*For Larissa*

# CONTENTS

# FOREWORD

After World War II, my family moved from New York City to neighboring Long Island. Many of the city's eight million people, having lived through the Depression and the war, were ready to live the American dream in the new suburbs that were springing up beyond the city's crowded five boroughs.

My father was one of the many postwar builders to come out from the city to create this new suburban frontier amid the farms, forests, and Colonial-era villages of old Long Island. By the end of the next decade, over one million people had transformed much of Long Island's two rural counties into suburbia.

I recall as a child my father taking me with him as he rode around the new housing tracts in his Army-surplus jeep. Even at that young age, I comprehended that I was seeing the end of an old way of life and the beginning of something new.

Later, as I was growing into adulthood on Long Island, I came to know and understand the early Dutch and English history of the island dating back to the 1600s, and I realized there was much that should have been preserved. At the time, there was an urgency to provide homes to returning veterans and their baby boomer families, so questions of land use, ecology, and landmark preservation were not on anyone's agenda.

The builders first bought up the farms and grazing lands of the Hempstead Plains, which were perfect for large subdivisions, and then they bought and cleared the scattered forests. The North Shore of Long Island, however, was more of a challenge. This is the Gold Coast, a hilly terrain along the Long Island Sound that was home to dozens of old villages and almost 1,200 estates, ranging from impressive to magnificent. Eventually, the economic and social realities of the postwar and post-Depression world made these estates untenable for their owners, and many of them were sold to developers.

The great houses—some containing over a hundred rooms—began falling to the wrecker's ball, and the landscaped grounds were divided into building lots. Much of the visible evidence of what was once the largest collection of wealth, power, and grand homes in America was disappearing.

By the mid-1970s, destruction had slowed, and efforts were being made to preserve the remaining estates as museums, parks, institutions, or nature conservancies.

Today, about 400 estates are still in private lands, so one can still imagine this privileged and opulent world as it once existed in the years throughout the Gilded Age, the Jazz Age of the Roaring Twenties, up through the stock market crash of 1929 and beyond, until World War II finally brought to a close this unique chapter of American history.

Paul Mateyunas, in *Long Island's Gold Coast*, has done a wonderful job of collecting and capturing the images and the feeling of this era, and though many of these magnificent mansions are gone, we can still marvel at them here on these pages.

—Nelson DeMille
author, *The Gold Coast*

# ACKNOWLEDGMENTS

This book could not have been made possible without the help of all the photographers, living and dead, who captured our homes and way of life, and the families and individuals who have shared their stories with me: Lindsay and Joan Anderson; Chad Brisbane; J. Hays Browning; Chris Collora for the idea for this book; Nelson and Sandy DeMille; Bonnie Devendorf of Daniel Gale; Dian Dunn; Jim and Diane Eckel; Geoffrey K. Fleming; Gina Frantellizzi for photo editing the images for this book; Joan Harrison; Abby Henry; Aleta Heisig; Warren Kraft; Jon P. and Loretta Mateyunas; Nancy Melius; Scott Neher; Ursula C. and William Niarakis; Melody Penna; Paul and Cecily Pennoyer; Howard and Mary Phipps; Linda Moore Post; Joel Post; Charles and Shirley Riker; Carolyn and Bobby Sessa; Larissa M. Szczupak; Avery Library, Columbia University; Myrna Sloam, Bryant Library; Dr. Katherine A. Schwab, Fairfield University Art History Department; Karen Martin, Huntington Historical Society; Society for the Preservation of Long Island Antiquities; and Lance Reinheimer and Florence Ogg, the Suffolk County Vanderbilt Museum. Each caption title includes the name of the house or image, year of construction, or, if it is an image with people, year of take. Images and information are courtesy of the following collections and periodicals:

(AA) *The American Architect* magazine
(A&D) *Arts & Decoration* magazine
(AF) *Architectural Forum* magazine
(AR) *Architectural Record* magazine
(ARCH) *Architecture* magazine
(BAR) *American Estates and Gardens*
(BB) *Brickbuilder* magazine
(BFA) Browning Family Album
(BL) Bryant Library, Local History Collection, Roslyn New York
(BR) Brother Roman
(CL) *Country Life* magazine
(EFA) Eckel Family Album
(H&G) *House & Garden* magazine
(HH) Huntington Historical Society
(GOTT) Avery Library, Columbia University

(HOW) *Noted Long Island Homes*
(LIS) Long Island Studies Institute
(LOC) Library of Congress
(MM) *Mansions & Millionaires*, Arlene Travis & Carole Aronson
(PAT) *American Homes of To-Day*
(PC) Private Collection
(PFA) Pennoyer Family Album
(PGC) Private Gottscho Collection
(PJM) Collection of author
(RFA) Rumsey Family Album
(SPLIA) Society for the Preservation of Long Island Antiquities
(T&C) *Town & Country* magazine
(WD) William Dozer
(VAN) Suffolk County Vanderbilt Museum

# INTRODUCTION

Long Island has a unique topography of wetlands, beaches, deep woods, rolling hills, and flat plains nestled between the sandy beaches of the Atlantic Ocean to the south and the deep protected harbors of Long Island Sound to the north. Formed by glaciers around 19,000 BC, it is the largest island in the contiguous United States. This gateway to New York City comprised of rural farms and small seaport villages was relatively quiet until the turn of the 20th century; however, when the automobile cut the journey from Manhattan to less then an hour, wealthy New Yorkers looking for a restful place to get out of the bustling city discovered the untouched North Shore. From then on, the countryside was transformed.

Throughout history, prosperity and wealth have flourished side by side with art and culture. During the Renaissance in Florence, Italy, the Medicis and other ruling families built the Duomo, Pitti Palace, and the Uffizi. They filled these great structures with works of art by Michelangelo, Raphael, and Bernini. At the beginning of the 20th century, Long Island's North Shore held one of the greatest concentrations of wealth in the nation. The families of this area were connected to every major industry in the world, including railroads, mining, banking, and shipping. The result of this great prosperity was a modern renaissance, bringing with it great buildings and art in a concentrated area, which became known as the Gold Coast.

The first houses began to appear around 1890 along the shoreline in towns like Manhasset, Glen Cove, Oyster Bay, and Huntington, with vast inland estates developing just north of the Hempstead Plains in what is now Old Westbury. As roads improved, the convenient locale prospered, and a building boom occurred. The result was a flourishing community boasting over 1,200 estates that stretched from the western shoreline of Great Neck to Eaton's Neck and south to Old Westbury. As the number of estates grew, new villages formed around them, and towns like Port Washington, Westbury, and Syosset split up to form Sands Point, Old Westbury, and Muttontown.

Summer activities on the Gold Coast and its residents were often featured in the news. The area was popularized in the social pages of the day and immortalized in *The Great Gatsby*, F. Scott Fitzgerald's famous novel. Muses for his book, such as the villages of Sands Point and Kings Point (fictionalized as East Egg and West Egg), along with a number of the large estates, provided inspiration for the homes of characters such as Daisy Buchanan and Jay Gatsby.

Top architects and decorators from the United States and Europe were responsible for dreaming up designs and filling these homes with the finest antiques, art, and furniture. They were sent on extensive trips to Europe for inspiration and to collect architectural elements, garden ornaments, or paneled rooms to incorporate. Ashbel H. Barney, son of the president of Knickerbocker Trust, took an entire château. Purchasing the 18th-century dwelling outside Dijon, he had it crated and shipped to Upper Brookville then reassembled under the supervision of Locust Valley architect Pleasants Pennington. The Château des Thons remains privately owned. Most did not take it as far as Barney, though nearly every style of architecture was represented. Louis Comfort Tiffany's farm at Laurel Hollow resembled a Moorish village, while his neighbor Mortimer Schiff had an Tudor that was later replaced by a château. Others created new uniquely American styles.

Landscape architects, such as Frederick Law Olmsted of Olmsted & Vaux (responsible for New York's Central Park) and his sons' firm, the Olmsted Brothers, would transform the field of landscape design by creating an American landscape style with over 100 Long Island commissions. Some of the first female landscape architects, Marian Cruger Coffin and Beatrix Ferrand designed gardens at Caumsett for Marshal Field III and Oheka for Otto H. Kahn. Some had private golf courses, like Isaac Guggenheim's house at Sands Point, rumored to have been built after his application to a local club was rejected. In Glen Cove, Capt. Joseph DeLamar's 82-room Pembroke had an entire indoor botanical garden, which cost an estimated $500,000 to construct in 1914 and was considered the largest private conservatory in the world. At the center of this tropical paradise was a luxurious round, mosaic-tile swimming pool, and on its lower level, a private screening room, squash court, and rifle range. At the Tudor-style Chimneys in Sands Point, Christian Holmes had an elaborate basement filled with a totem-pole bar, swimming pool, shooting gallery, squash court, and a bowling alley, all decorated in a Southwestern Art Deco theme with murals by Gardner Hale. A number of estates had entire recreational buildings, called playhouses or casinos, with indoor pools and tennis courts. Much like at the Chimneys, they were often whimsical in their designs and devoted to their owners' every fantasy.

While the great stock market crash of 1929 affected much of the country, contrary to popular belief it did not have a large impact on the lives of those who owned these Long Island country houses. Many families continued to live their lives much as before, and smaller-scale estate houses were built. The area prospered until the end of World War II, when staff shortages, increasing costs, and population growth created the need for housing. Communities, such as Levittown, sprang up and forever changed the country landscape.

Modern highways built by Robert Moses also changed the landscape. Delayed at first, Old Westbury estate owners successfully campaigned to divert the Northern State Parkway away from the village and their large properties. The solution became known as Objectors' Bend, which is the sudden, almost 90-degree turn south on the parkway as one approaches Old Westbury from the west. The path of the Long Island Expressway was their second battle and caused much debate, as Robert Moses's plans called for the expressway to cut through the middle of places like the village of Old Westbury. The estate owners were not victorious, and the expressway divided villages and estates in half. Places like J. Cornelius Rathborne's Pelican Farm were razed, and William P. Thompson's and F. Skiddy von Stade's driveways from Jericho Turnpike were divided in half, with several picturesque allées of trees starting on one side of the expressway and ending on the other.

By the 1950s, the houses were out of fashion, many estate owners had died, and their fortunes were divided or lost. So daunting were the costs of maintenance, many of the main houses were left empty and unheated, the roofs leaked, and gardens became overgrown. Homes were left abandoned for years and ended up in ruin, making demolition the only viable option. This continued through the 1960s and 1970s, when the majority of estates were broken up and developed.

The real estate booms of the 1980s and early 2000s proved to be an interesting time for the Gold Coast estates. While land values soared and available building lots were scarce, it was no longer a maintenance issue, but an issue of the bottom line. The land was worth more than the house, so more homes were razed. Simultaneously, another, smaller trend to restore these houses formed as a result of changing zoning laws and construction costs. For some buyers, the houses were now undervalued. The restrictions on new-construction square footage and height made the old homes, which were indeed well designed and built to last, both impossible to reproduce and, once updated, cost-effective. Today, approximately one third of the historic estates remain, with several houses still disappearing each year.

**MODERN FARM BUILDINGS, 1918.**
Many of the estates continued
Long Island's agricultural history by
constructing large working farms
on the property. Architect Alfred
E. Hopkins gained prominence as
the go-to architect for designing
working farms that complemented
the architecture of the main house.
Hopkins's work could be seen on
dozens of properties along the
North Shore, including those of
Louis Comfort Tiffany, George S.
Brewster, and Marshall Field. (CL.)

**HARBOR HILL DAIRY, 1900–1902.**
Warren & Wetmore, the same
firm that designed Manhattan's
Grand Central Terminal,
designed the dairy at Clarence H.
Mackay's Harbor Hill in Roslyn.
Housing his prize Guernseys,
Mackay's 648-acre compound
was complete with separate
horse and polo pony stables, dog
kennels, farmworker lodgings,
and numerous workshops. (BL.)

# One

# LIFE ON THE NORTH SHORE

**STAFF AT HARBOR HILL.** During its heyday, a staff of over 180 people worked at Harbor Hill to maintain the house and grounds. Until World War II, country estates on the North Shore were run like their English counterparts. They would often have 30 to 100 on staff and operate like small hotels in the summer season. Pictured here, an unidentified inside maid from Harbor Hill goes for a ride. Designed by McKim, Mead, & White, Harbor Hill construction began in 1899 and took nearly three years to complete. (BL.)

MOTOR'S GALLERY OF MOTORING

No. 1. William K. Vanderbilt, Jr.

ONE MILE IN SECONDS. AVERAGE OVER 92 MILES AN HOUR. ORMOND-DAYTONA FLA. JAN. 27, 1904

HOLDING THE SPEED RECORD FOR THIS EARTH, THE
CHAMPION SEEKS OTHER WORLDS TO CONQUER

**BREAKING THE SPEED RECORD, 1904.**
William K. Vanderbilt Jr., sportsman, heir to the New York Central Railroad fortune, and one of Long Island's fastest residents, constructed a private parkway that stretched 45 miles from Flushing, New York, to Lake Ronkonkoma. It became a private toll road in the 1920s and was a speeding-ticket-free way for many of the residents to get to the North Shore from Manhattan. (VAN.)

**AT THE FINISH LINE, 1905.**
Willie K. Vanderbilt Jr. and his sister Consuelo, the former Duchess of Marlborough, are pictured at the finish line of the Vanderbilt Motor Cup races. Started in 1904, the races were a popular sight of the day. Attracting huge crowds, the events became too dangerous and ended in 1910. Vanderbilt sold his interests in the parkway in 1938, and several stretches of the parkway are still in use today. (VAN.)

**WILLIE OFF NEW LONDON, 1898.**
A popular activity of the day, boating
was a way of life for many residents. It
would not be unusual during the summer
to see a variety of vessels on Long Island
Sound or in the harbors. Many yacht
clubs held races, and Vanderbilt dubbed
one of his racers *Hard Boiled Egg*, because
according to him, "like a hard-boiled
egg, it could not be beaten." (VAN.)

**THE *ALVA*, 1931.** Named for his
mother, William K. Vanderbilt Jr.'s
260-foot-long *Alva* was designed
by Cox and Stevens. It could often
be seen anchored off his home,
Eagle's Nest, in Northport Bay, or
cruising around the world to collect
marine specimens for his private
marine museum, which he regularly
opened to the public. Upon his
death, Vanderbilt willed his home
to Suffolk County as a museum,
which still operates. (VAN.)

**HUSSAR, 1923.** Pictured is the second Mrs. E.F. (Marjorie Merriweather Post) Hutton's 200-foot *Hussar*. A floating palace, it was decorated by the popular William Baumgarten & Co. The living room reflected 18th-century English motifs and had a working fireplace decorated as finely as her Brookville home, Hillwood (page 60). Mrs. Post commissioned a number of boats over her lifetime. Like J.P. Morgan Jr. with his *Corsair*, Post donated her yachts to aid the US war effort. After military service, Post's later yacht, the *Sea Cloud*, was used as a storage barge in South America until a group of German investors purchased and restored it for use as a charter vessel. It now serves as a reminder for many of the cruising golden age. (Both, T&C.)

COMMUTERS, 1930 AND 1927. As the North Shore became more than a summer residence for New York businessmen, motorboats dubbed "commuters" became a popular way for people to get to their offices in Manhattan. The cartoon above, featured in a 1930 society paper, is titled *Rush Hour at the New York Yacht Club*. It was thought to be the modern, more relaxing way to deal with Long Island's growing population and traffic. Men like Morgan, Pratt, Pennoyer, and Field utilized this method of commuting. Local members could leave from Glen Cove's New York Yacht Club (NYYC) Station 10, erected in 1904 in what is now Morgan Park. Their course set for the NYYC East River landing station at Twenty-sixth Street, pictured below. (Above, PC; below, CL.)

**NASSAU COUNTRY CLUB, 1910.** Located in Glen Cove, the Nassau Country Club opened its doors in 1898 as an outgrowth of the Queens County Club and was organized by residents of the nearby North Country Colony. The clubhouse, designed by Woodruff Leeming in 1910, replaced the original Shingle Style clubhouse destroyed by a fire in 1909. The Tudor-style structure was built by the J. Dall Co., and the club still operates from this building today. (ARCH.)

**THE CREEK CLUB, 1923.** The club was constructed on the site of New York attorney Paul Cravath's estate, Veraton. The house was lost twice to fire; after the second time in 1914, Cravath sold the land and build on nearby Duck Pond Road. The club utilized Cravath's original massive tree-lined driveway and built a brick clubhouse designed by Walker & Gillette in 1923. It remains a private club. (PJM.)

**THE PRIVATE HANGER, 1929.** As the trend for flying became popular in late 1920s, Long Island boasted one of the first aviation clubs. Opening in the summer of 1929 shortly before the stock market crash, it survived less than two decades before being sold to William Levitt, who transformed its grounds into Levittown. The proposed "home hanger," designed by Chester B. Price, was featured in *House & Garden* magazine and thought to be an approaching necessity. If not for World War II, many estates might have had private hangers. (H&G.)

**SANDS POINT CASINO, 1925.** A place for bathing, dancing, yachting, and weekly clambakes, the bath club, designed by Kenneth M. Murchison in the Mediterranean style, was located at the northwestern edge of Sands Point. It boasted everything a member interested in the beach could desire, including, as described by the architect, "35 gaily colored cabanas" reminiscent of Venice dotting the shoreline. Of several original clubs in Sands Point, only the Sands Point Golf Club still exists. The bath club was lost to fire in 1986. (PJM.)

**JAY PHIPPS WITH HIS BEAGLES, 1913.** A member of the Meadowbrook Hunt, founded in 1881, Phipps is pictured here at his estate, Westbury House. Rivaled only by the Rockaway Hunt, the Meadowbrook Hunt was the dominant hunt club on the North Shore, and members could often be seen galloping through Old Westbury, Muttontown, and as far east as Oyster Bay. Its roster included Pres. Theodore Roosevelt, Tommy Hitchcock, and Mrs. Francis P. (Mabel) Garvan. (T&C.)

**THE ARROW, 1946.** Among the many equestrian activities on the North Shore, coaching was popular. Here, noted equestrian F. Ambrose Clark of Old Westbury is seen on his road coach, *The Arrow*, in the forecourt of his home, Broad Hollow. Clark is coachman, with Harry St. Clair Zogbaum, James Cooley, Frederic H. Price Jr., Arthur Parrett, and Jack Grace as guards. Horses Moet and Chandon are wheelers; Nina de Polignac and Widow Cliquot are leaders. (PJM.)

**BABYLON HORSE SHOW, 1923.** At the wheel is Katherine Redmond of Upper Brookville (page 92), with M.L. Baird (left) and Barbara Register. One of the most popular activities at the time, horse shows were held at Meadowbrook, Piping Rock, Sands Point, Cedar Valley Farm, and Caumsett, just to name a few. (T&C.)

**MEADOWBROOK CUP, SEPTEMBER 1927.** The noted Meadowbrook Club had one of the most successful runs of polo victories in US history. By the 1920s, polo was becoming a big-league sport with upwards of 20,000 to 30,000 spectators at the Meadowbrook fields watching from the club's signature robin's egg–blue stands. Losing popularity during World War II, the Meadowbrook grounds were sold in 1954. Today, the fields are the site of parking lots and warehouse stores just south of Old Country Road in Westbury. (CL.)

**FOOTMEN AND BUTLER AT HARBOR HILL, 1907.** Clarence Mackay's home was the site of many grand celebrations. Upon a visit from the Prince of Wales to the Meadowbrook Club during the International Polo Matches of 1924, Mackay hosted a ball in his honor for 1,200 guests, with a who's who guest list. Thousands of colored lights could be seen from Roslyn Harbor. With Mackay's fortune dwindling, the home was closed in 1932 and razed in 1947. (BL.)

**DRIVER AT LAUREL ACRES, 1924.** Pictured are a chauffeur and a gentleman (both unidentified) in the motor court of the Frederick L. Lutz home at Oyster Bay. Named Laurel Acres, the 11,000-square-foot stucco home was designed by Locust Valley architect Harrie T. Lindeberg. The most noticeable feature is the decorative metal transom arch and surround of the entrance executed by Oscar Bach. It features a number of Lindeberg's signature woodland-creature designs. The home survives in private hands. (EFA.)

FETE AT BOSCOBEL, DATE UNKNOWN. Pictured is an unknown theatrical performance at Horatio S. Shonnard's water gardens. Architect Donn Barber joined the best of both water and land vistas in a stunning and unique environment intrinsic to Long Island. Boscobel's gardens combined water, fragrant and colorful flowers, white gravel walking paths, towering specimen trees, earthy stone walls, and statuary. The sunken gardens were bound by the natural slope of the land and were divided into three parts, designed in succession, so all would overlook Oyster Bay. For decoration and amusement, a stylized boat landing hosted an elaborate Venetian gondola that was used during special musical performances. When the estate was subdivided, the majority of the gardens were destroyed, and the final section was replaced with a Japanese-style garden by one of the new homeowners of the subdivision. (Both, PJM.)

**IN RESIDENCE AT BEAUPRE, 1948.** In 1948, the Duke and Duchess of Windsor took up residence on the North Shore at several houses—sometimes rent-free. They are pictured here at the Lattingtown home, owned at the time by Brooks Howe. Walker & Gillette designed the estate, which bordered the Creek Club, in 1932 for T. Suffern Tailer. The Windsors also resided at Evelyn Marshall Field's Easton in Muttontown. (PC.)

**WEDDING AT THE BRAES, 1923.** In 1923, Herbert L. Pratt's daughter Harriet married Lawrence Bell Van Ingen. She is pictured here with her bridesmaids on the back terrace of her father's home, The Braes, now the Webb Institute in Glen Cove. The young couple was given Preference, a comfortable brick Georgian-style mansion designed by Carrère & Hastings in 1924. It remains a private home. (T&C.)

**LINDA MOORE AT CHELSEA, 1930S.** Linda, daughter of Alexandra Moore McKay, is pictured here dressed as an apple blossom princess on the back terrace of her parents' Muttontown home. Not just about social parties, the North Shore had many family activities and events. Every Sunday at Chelsea was a lunch of family and friends, where the children sometimes dressed in costume. (PJM.)

**CHILDREN AT HARBOR HILL COACH STABLE, C. 1910.** The children of families who were employed at Harbor Hill and other estates often had fond memories of their childhood. Before the era of employee benefits, many of the estate owners took good care of their staff by paying doctors' bills, educating their children, and treating them to special parties. At E.D. Morgan's Old Westbury home, a winter Christmas carnival was held in the ballroom, with as many as 60 of the staff's children in attendance. (BL.)

**BUILDING THE GOLD COAST, FAIRLEIGH, 1914.** Around 1910, the country-house era was in full swing, and teams of workers spent an average of two years to complete an estate. Men like Otto Kahn and Marshall Field employed nearly 1,000 men to build their homes. Kahn even created the Cold Spring Harbor Railroad Station to bring the men to his property. Here, construction begins at Fairleigh in Muttontown. (MM.)

**FAIRLEIGH UNDER CONSTRUCTION, 1914.** Standard Oil heir George S. Brewster used Westover Plantation, in Virginia, to serve as a model for his summer home. Encompassing 35,000 square feet, the house was designed by Trowbridge & Livingston, with grounds by James L. Greenleaf and a farm complex by Alfred E. Hopkins. Today, the farm group survives as one of the largest intact farms by Hopkins in Nassau County. (MM.)

# *Two*

# THE HOUSES

**FAIRLEIGH, ENTRANCE FRONT, 1914–1916.** For the limestone entrance surround and Palladian window, Trowbridge was inspired by Philadelphia's Independence Hall. Of the original 195 acres, 155 remain as Hoffman Center, a private foundation that saved the property from becoming a 57-home subdivision. Ransacked and stripped of its original details prior to the purchase by Hoffman Center, the home has been fully restored to its 1916 condition. (MM.)

**MARTIN HALL, 1900.** The 35-acre waterfront estate of James E. Martin was located at the western end of Kings Point looking toward Fort Totten. Completed in 1900 by Little & O'Connor, the house boasted a tremendous two-story portico supported by Ionic columns and elaborate gardens by the Olmsted Brothers. The house was demolished two years after this photograph was taken in 1932. (PJM.)

**SOUTHWICK RESIDENCE AT GREAT NECK, 1927.** Pictured is the Tudor-style home of C.T. Southwick, designed by Arthur W. Coote, an architect with the firm Tooker & Marsh. Combining a variety of materials into the design, Coote utilized brick, stucco, slate, and timber in its construction. The modestly scaled home was not scant on details, which featured a barrel-vaulted ceiling in the sunken living room and a carved stone fireplace. The status of this home, later purchased by Carroll Earle, is unknown. (AF.)

MARY RUMSEY HOUSE, 1927. After the death of her husband, Charles Cary Rumsey, in 1922, Mary purchased five waterfront acres at the eastern tip of Sands Point and left her Old Westbury home (page 64). She hired the renowned firm McKim, Mead, & White, with Mead to execute the plans. The new residence, an imposing château, was the perfect compliment to neighboring Beacon Towers, seen on the cover and at the far left of this photograph. Lived in by the Rumsey family for two generations virtually untouched, it was put on the market for $9.9 million in 2011, selling in 2012. (RFA.)

SANDS POINT BEACH HOUSE, 1932. Modest in scale describes the first summer home of Averell Harriman, which overlooked Long Island Sound. Commissioned by the future 48th governor of New York in the early 1930s, architect James W. O'Connor collaborated with landscape architect Louise Payson to design it to be a practical and comfortable beachside residence. With the market crash of 1929, increasing taxes, and changing styles, manageable homes like Harriman's became more and more fashionable. (H&G.)

CASTLE GOULD STABLES, 1902. Pictured is a view from the main house to the stables at Castle Gould, built for Howard Gould, son of railroad tycoon Jay Gould. In its heyday, over 200 workers helped maintain the nearly 400-acre Sands Point estate. Modeled after Kilkenny Castle in Ireland, the stable was designed by Augustus N. Allen and is roughly 60,000 square feet. Visible to the right is the Gould kennel. (PJM.)

HEMPSTEAD HOUSE, 1909–1911. The main house at Castle Gould was built in the Gothic style and considered to be "the most livable large house in America," according to *Architecture* magazine. Gould's ownership was short-lived. He sold it fully furnished just eight years after completion, in 1917, to Daniel Guggenheim. Guggenheim thought it was quite a bargain, considering since both of their names started with G, he did not have to change the initial on the gates, silver, or bed linens. (ARCH.)

**MILLE FLEURS, 1931.** After Daniel Guggenheim's death in 1930, his wife, Florence, thought Hempstead House was too large and unmanageable. She hired Polhemus & Coffin to construct a smaller home with the majority of the rooms, including the bedrooms, on a single level. Located on the southern side of the estate, Mille Fleurs, like its name suggested, was surrounded by many flower gardens, including a walled garden that was enclosed by the U-shaped house. (HOW.)

**FALAISE, 1923.** Capt. Harry Guggenheim and his bride moved into Falaise in 1923. It sat on 90 acres, which were gifted to him by his parents as a wedding present and were formerly part of Hempstead House's private golf course. The home truly is, as its French name implies, at the cliff's edge, as it was literally built into a bluff overlooking the Sound. Today, all of the Guggenheim homes are part of the Nassau County–owned park, the Sands Point Preserve. (PJM.)

**THE F. SCOTT FITZGERALDS, 1923.**
Writer F. Scott Fitzgerald and his wife,
Zelda, are pictured two years before the
publication of *The Great Gatsby*. The
couple lived in Great Neck from 1922
until 1924. Keewaydin, pictured below,
is said to be one of the inspirations for
Daisy Buchanan's home in the novel.
It is quite possible that the house, a
landmark at the entrance of Hempstead
Harbor, influenced the writer. (T&C.)

**KEEWAYDIN UNDER CONSTRUCTION,**
**1911–1913.** Pictured is the home
of clothier John Scott Browning
under construction. In August 1910,
Browning purchased 11 acres of land,
then known as Prospect Point, and
named the house Keewaydin, which
is an Algonquin word for "northwest
wind." The home was completed by late
1912, followed by the gardens in 1913.
Although the architect is unknown,
the home is often attributed to the firm
of McKim, Mead, & White. (BFA.)

APPROACH TO KEEWAYDIN, 1911–1913. The Brownings enjoyed their summerhouse, which was the center of family activity, and their pack of nearly one dozen Great Danes. John's brother had a pet monkey who traveled with him everywhere. Once, when his brother came to visit, the dogs caught sight of the monkey from across the property. Startled, the monkey leapt from the Browning's shoulder, climbed to the top of the roof, and began ripping out roof tiles and throwing them at the dogs as they galloped down the driveway. Browning died in 1919, and the home was rented and sold by 1923. During its time for sale, the house was renamed Kidd's Rock. In 1929, publisher Herbert Swope acquired the property and occupied the home until 1962. (Both, BFA.)

**GREENTREE, 1903 AND POOL, 1914.** Greentree was the Manhasset estate of William Payne Whitney and, later, his son John Hay Whiney. It encompassed most of the land from the Long Island Expressway to Northern Boulevard, between Shelter Rock Road and Community Drive. The original home was constructed in 1903 by d'Hautville & Cooper and altered several times. The largest change occurred in 1914 with the addition of a tennis court building by T. Markoe Robertson. The lower level consisted of an indoor pool, steam rooms, and men's and ladies' dressing rooms. On the floor above, there was an indoor tennis court, six guest rooms, and wood paneled sitting rooms. A residence for nearly a century, upon Mrs. John Hay (Betsey Cushing) Whitney's death in 1998, the home and its 408 acres were transferred to the Greentree Foundation, which, like the Whitneys, rarely opens the house to photographers or the public. (Both, ARCH.)

**WHITNEY BOATHOUSE, 1929.** After inheriting Greentree from his father, John Hay Whitney constructed this boathouse just north of the estate with the help of Christopher Grant La Farge. The structure was designed to hold all of Whitney's sporting novelties, including his amphibious airplane. The interiors included a whimsical, nautically themed club room of 50-by-30 feet facing a large, open porch overlooking the bay and an open third-floor deck for sunbathing. There were also four guest rooms and separate dressing rooms to freshen up after a day at sea. The boathouse was sold upon Whitney's death in 1982 and converted to a residence. (Both, AA.)

**BROOKWOOD, 1929.** One of Thomas H. Ellett's last North Shore commissions was the Manhasset home of Henry M. and Helen C. Minton. It was named for the brook that ran through the property and for the woods where it was constructed off New Hyde Park Road. The nine-acre estate reflected picturesque French details, with its delicate iron balconies and ornamental dormer pediments. The estate was sold in 1980, subdivided, and demolished. (HOW.)

**INISFADA, 1916–1920.** Meaning "long island" in Gaelic, Inisfada was the home of Nicholas and Genevieve Brady. Upon its completion in 1920, it was the fourth-largest home in the country. Architect John Torrey Windrim crowned the Elizabethan-style house with 37 different patterned chimneys. A widow of seven years with no children, Genevieve Brady donated the estate in 1937 to the Society of Jesus, which still operates it as the St. Ignatius Retreat House. (PC.)

BROOKHOLT AND DINING ROOM, 1897. In 1897, two years after her divorce from William K. Vanderbilt Sr. and a year after her marriage to Oliver Hazard Perry Belmont, Alva hired her favorite architect, Richard Morris Hunt, to design her new country house at Hempstead. Brookholt was an elaborate wooden house modeled in the French Neoclassical style. The interiors featured lavishly decorated rooms with oversized French casement windows and elaborate plasterwork. Furnished in a mix of French and English appointments with large portraits hanging from the walls, the dining room had richly cast moldings and pilasters, with one wall adorned with a cast of the Belmont coat of arms. On the second floor, there was a vast arched gallery hall open to the stairs that displayed artwork, which covered most of the available walls. By 1950, the area had been developed and the house demolished. (Both, PC.)

**L.H. SHERMAN HOUSE, 1918.** L.H. Sherman, the first mayor of North Hills and a prominent attorney, constructed this large brick and Indiana sandstone Tudor. Sherman hired James W. O'Connor to design the home, which sat on nearly 60 acres bordering what was then the Links Golf Club. Sherman sold the house in 1929, and by 1950, it was converted for use as the Buckley Country Day School. (H&G.)

**STONEHOUSE, 1868, 1906.** Set high atop Roslyn Harbor, the 1868 home of yachtsman Thomas Clapham was named for the granite of which it was constructed. Originally designed by Jacob Wrey Mould, the house underwent several transformations in both name and appearance, the view above reflects the 1906 updating of the house from Victorian Gothic to a less ornamented Château-style. The second owner, Benjamin Stern, renamed the house Claraben Court. A fire in the 1960s further simplified the facade, and today it remains privately owned. (PJM.)

**BRYCE HOUSE AND DINING ROOM, 1901.** Setting out to build a country house, paymaster general and state congressman of New York Lloyd Stevens Bryce purchased a tract of land from William Cullen Bryant that overlooked Hempstead Harbor and hired Ogden Codman Jr. to design the house. Childs Frick, son of Carnegie Steel partner Henry Frick, and his growing family purchased the estate in 1919 and renamed it Clayton. The Fricks expanded the gardens with the help of Marian Cruger Coffin and hired London-based Sir Charles Carrick Allom to remodel the home. The Fricks lived there until Childs's death in 1965. It was sold to Nassau County in 1969, and today the main house is open to the public as the Nassau County Museum of Art. (Both, BAR.)

ENTRANCE TO JOHN W. MACKAY HOUSE, 1929. Across Glen Cove Road from Clarence H. Mackay's Harbor Hill, his son John constructed this home in 1929. The work of John Walter Cross of Cross & Cross, the English Cotswold–style home was a compact version of his father's estate and encompassed a garage, cottage, kennel, stable at its entrance, a field with a dog run, a barn for sheep, gardens, and a swimming pool on 28 acres. Built to be fireproof, the home was constructed from Indiana sandstone with a slate roof. To achieve an aged look, the stone was sandblasted, the lead-coated copper leaders and gutters antiqued, and the oak woodwork hand-hewn. Thought to be a truly modern design, the grounds could be maintained by a single man with minimal staff needed inside. Today, the farm group and house stand as private residences. (Both, PJM.)

ROSLYN HALL, 1891. James Brown Lord designed this eclectic 60-room, half-timber house for Wall Street broker Stanley Mortimer at the age of 32. In 1919, it was sold to Francis P. Garvan, whose sister Genevieve Brady was nearing completion on her own Manhasset home, Inisfada (page 34). The Garvans expanded the gardens extensively, with help from the Olmsted Brothers. The home was demolished in 1974, but several rooms and gardens have been incorporated into modern homes on the grounds. (PJM.)

OLD ACRES, 1909. American statesman and diplomat Robert L. Bacon Sr. hired noted architect John Russell Pope to design Old Acres, located in Old Westbury. Finished in shingle, the central wing of the house was flanked by protruding side wings, which formed a walled motor court. In 1915, Pope returned to Old Westbury to design a similar house for Bacon's son Robert Jr. Old Acres was taken down in 1960, and only the son's house remains. (PJM.)

**STABLES AT BROAD HOLLOW, 1912.** F. Ambrose Clark, or "Brose" as friends knew him, lived at Broad Hollow with his wife, Florence. Both were avid riders, and she was cited by *Time* magazine as being a model sportswoman. Clark, a partner of the Singer Sewing Machine Company, was master of the hounds at the Meadowbrook Hunt through the 1920s and a founder of the Country Lanes Committee, a group with miles of bridle paths through Nassau County. His thoroughbred stable, with its pale-blue-and-yellow racing silks, had a lifespan of 60 years. The 400-acre compound at Old Westbury was ideal for horses; the majority of the land was flat for paddocks, with rolling hills and deep woods for riding. Most of his neighbors were sportsmen, such as Tyler Morse, Devereux Milburn, and Robert Winthrop. (Both, PC.)

**BROAD HOLLOW REAR FACADE, 1912.** From the arched brick and limestone gatehouse on what is now the North Service Road of the Long Island Expressway, the long, tree-lined drive made a sharp left to reveal a large, flat lawn, punctuated by a raised terrace on which the Clarks' 60-room Georgian home stood. Most striking was the two-story Doric-columned portico. The drive continued past the stables and turned right up a mild incline to the front of the house, which had a more human-scaled, single-story entrance porch. The stair hall rose two stories and through the depth of the house, opening to the portico and vast fields. The Clarks divided their time between Broad Hollow and their farms in Cooperstown, New York; Aiken, South Carolina; and Melton, Mowbray, England, as well as the Dakota on Central Park West, built by Clark's father. Upon Ambrose Clark's death in 1964, Broad Hollow was willed to the State University of New York, which while converting the house for campus use accidentally lost it to fire. (Both, PC.)

**MORSE LODGE, 1909–1910.** Tyler Morse purchased a tract of land and an old house that Little & Browne would renovate from 1909 until 1910. A Boston attorney, Tyler and his wife, Allon Fuller, divided their time between Manhattan, Palm Beach, and Old Westbury. Passionate for dogs, the couple bred English sheepdogs, with several Westminster winners. Allon Fuller died at 37, leaving half of her $4-to-5-million estate to Tyler with the stipulation that he would lose it all if he remarried. The house remains under private ownership. (PJM.)

**BENNETT COTTAGE, 1910.** George Rose, heir to his father's Royal Baking Powder Company, commissioned Hoppin & Koen to design his house. Located on 50 acres in Old Westbury, the home had 12 family bedrooms, 6 baths, and 12 staff bedrooms. A fire destroyed it in 1952, and the property was subsequently developed. (PC.)

Residence of Charles Steele, Westbury, L. I.

**STEELE HILL, 1891 AND ENTRANCE HALL, 1929.** Named Steele Hill by its second owner, the house was originally constructed by banker James F.D. Lanier and located on a hill off Post Road in Old Westbury. Completed in 1891, it was the second home designed by James Brown Lord on the North Shore. It was soon sold to Charles Steele, an attorney and a partner of J.P. Morgan. Steele put the house through several renovations. In the late 1920s, interior designer Elsie Cobb Wilson was hired to redecorate. Pictured is the entrance hall. After Steele's death, the estate was subdivided and the house razed in the late 1940s. Mrs. Charles (Nannie) Steele gave the 11 acres where the house stood as a wedding present to her grandson, who would build a house on the old foundation. (Both, PJM.)

**Von Stade House, 1914, 1930.** As wedding presents from the bride's parents, each of Charles Steele's daughters was given a parcel of land from the north end of Steele Hill. Kathryn wed first, to importer and polo player Francis Skiddy von Stade. Cross & Cross would design them a shingle farmhouse, which was doubled in size in 1930 by Old Westbury architect Julian Peabody, resulting in a sprawling Colonial of brick and shingle. (HOW.)

**Von Stade Library, 1930.** The interiors of the von Stade house reflected the couple's sporting interests. Above the fireplace is a painting of a von Stade thoroughbred, and displayed on the right windowsill is the bronze statue of Skiddy himself, which was sculpted by nearby resident, polo player, and artist Charles Cary Rumsey (page 64). Left in ruin for years by its last two owners, the von Stade house was razed and the property developed in 2012. (HOW.)

SUNRIDGE HALL, 1916. Nancy Steele married Devereux Milburn, and they built their home on 28 acres adjoining the property of her sister Kathryn von Stade. Julian Peabody designed Sunridge Hall solidly out of stucco and brick. Milburn, an attorney and 10-goal polo player, was a member of a legendary team known as the Big Four, which included Harry Payne Whitney and brothers Lawrence and Monte Waterbury. Sunridge was partially razed, but a wing was converted to a smaller residence. (PAT.)

MAGPIES, 1923. Winners of the Meadowbrook Club Cup of 1923, the Magpies are, from left to right, William Goadby Loew, Devereux Milburn, C. Perry Beadleston, and Marshall Field III. Brothers-in-law Devereux Milburn and F. Skiddy von Stade were both active players with Meadowbrook and became hall of fame players, helping to make Meadowbrook legendary. (T&C.)

BROAD HOLLOW FARM, 1892–1893. Home of two of America's greatest polo players, Broad Hollow Farm is located off Jericho Turnpike in Old Westbury. The Thomas Hitchcocks resided in this early-1700s farmhouse remodeled in 1892 by architect Richard Morris Hunt. Hitchcock's son Tommy Hitchcock Jr. is the undisputed Babe Ruth of polo. In 1995, the estate was purchased by the Roman Catholic Diocese of Rockville Centre, which plans to convert it into a cemetery. (PJM.)

HOME ACRES, 1915. George and Martha Whitney commissioned Delano & Aldrich to build their Old Westbury home neighboring the bride's parents, Mr. and Mrs. Robert L. (Virginia Murray) Bacon Sr. (page 39). Whitney, a banker with J.P. Morgan, and his wife had four children. The family divided their time between a townhouse at 120 East Eightieth Street in Manhattan and Home Acres. The house remains a private residence. (HOW.)

**THE MANSE, 1899–1902** AND
**THE STUDIO, 1913.** At the turn
of the last century, financier and
politician William C. Whitney
amassed a compound of over 700
acres. After his death in 1904, his
son and daughter-in-law Harry Payne
and Gertrude Vanderbilt Whitney
took over the estate. The couple
called on McKim, Mead, & White,
who built the house, to make some
alterations in 1906–1910. They
called on Warren & Wetmore to add
the indoor pool and tennis house
(upper right), and then on Delano
& Aldrich to create a Palladian-
inspired studio for Gertrude, a
sculptress, to work. The studio (right)
was surrounded by formal gardens
and was complete with a furnace to
fire the finished works. The house
was razed in 1941 and 1942 by their
son Cornelius "Sonny" Vanderbilt
Whitney to make way for a more
manageable home by Beers &
Farley. (Above, A&D; right, PAT.)

**WHITNEY STABLE, 1898–1899 AND GLORIA AT STABLE, 1934.** Erected by William C. Whitney in 1899, the stable, according to the *Brooklyn Eagle*, was "the most wonderful stable in the world." Measuring 850 feet long, 60 feet wide, and over 100 feet across at its center, it boasted 83 stalls and took a team of 75 carpenters to construct. Below, 10-year-old Gloria Vanderbilt is pictured at the stable during the famous custody battle between her Aunt Gertrude and mother, Gloria Morgan Vanderbilt, after the death of her father, Reginald C. Vanderbilt. Gertrude was awarded custody, and Gloria attended the local Green Vale School. Gloria went on to launch a career in fashion and is mother to journalist Anderson Cooper. Today, the Whitney estate is divided in two major parcels: the stables, gymnasium, and several smaller houses make up the New York Institute of Technology campus, and the Whitney house and indoor tennis house are the Old Westbury Country Club. (Both, PJM.)

**FLORA WHITNEY HOUSE AND DINING ROOM, 1924.** Upon her marriage, Flora Whitney, Gertrude and Harry Payne Whitney's eldest daughter, was given a plot on her parents' estate to build a home. Flora would marry aviator and stockbroker Roderick Tower, but the marriage did not last, and the couple divorced shortly after the completion of the house. Designed by Delano & Aldrich, the French Château–style home was lived in by Flora and her second husband, G. Macculloch Miller III, whom she wed in 1927. Combining traditional style with slightly deco interiors, the home was decorated by Frankl Galleries. From 1941 until 1966, Flora served as president of the Whitney Museum of Art, which was founded by her mother. The house was sold in 1963 and used by the New York Institute of Technology until 1999, when it was sold again and later razed. (Above, HOW; below, PJM.)

IVYCROFT GATE LODGE, 1891–1894 AND FRONT FACADE, 1927. Originally built in 1891–1894 by Gage & Wallace for Perry Tiffany, the vice president of the Sterling Supply & Manufacturing Co., Ivycroft sat on 40 acres. Perry's grandfather was Commodore Perry, who opened Japan to the West. In 1925, architect Eliot B. Cross, of Cross & Cross, purchased and remodeled the estate for himself. Ivycroft underwent a second renovation to make it more manageable. The front and rear columned porches were removed, and the third floor and right wing were demolished. The house and gate lodge have been separated and are now private residences in Old Westbury. (PJM.)

**NEILSON HOUSE, 1910.** Little is known of Mrs. R.P. Neilson and her home at Old Westbury. Architect Algernon S. Bell, who was influenced by local Quaker farmhouses in designing the shingle home, constructed the estate in 1910. One walked through the small vestibule and up two steps to the main hall (below), where to the right were the dining room, kitchen, and staff rooms. To the left, the living room ran the full depth of the house, which opened up to the library with a corner fireplace. Through French doors opening from the library, a covered veranda led to the largest room in the house, a two-story vaulted studio. At the far end of the studio, a spiral staircase led to a balcony, open to the studio space with a Palladian window overlooking the garden. (Both, ARCH.)

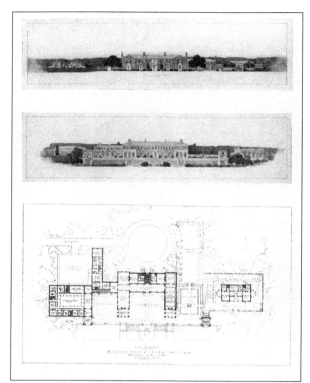

**GUINEA CHASE FARM, 1918.**
Hoppin & Koen erected the original Guinea Chase Farm in Wheatley Hills in 1906 for Mrs. J. Norman de R. (Vira Boarman) Whitehouse at a cost of $100,000. In 1915, the home and 73 acres were sold for $175,000 to Sidney S. Whelan. Shortly after, Whelan sought plans for a new house. The proposed plans, which were submitted by estate farm–group specialist Alfred E. Hopkins, were never executed. (ARCH.)

**MURRAY HOUSE, 1930.** The work of Dwight James Baum for John F. Murray in Old Westbury resulted in a Tudor-style home, which survives today in private hands. Murray, who was an engineer and commissioner of the Port Authority of New York under Gov. Franklin D. Roosevelt, died at the age of 37. (HOW.)

**BOXWOOD FARM, 1922.** Backing the polo fields in Old Westbury, Julian Peabody of Peabody, Wilson & Brown designed this house for Hugh Murray. Peabody was a nearby resident and had his own estate, Pond Hollow Farm, off Powells Lane. In 1936, Boxwood Farm was sold to polo player and insurance broker Charles V. Hickox. Both houses survive, but Peabody's house was altered beyond recognition in 1997. (CL.)

**BIG TREE FARM, 1917–1918.** Hidden behind a high brick wall on Wheatley Road sits Big Tree Farm, home of railroad magnate James N. Hill. Architects Walker & Gillette teamed up with the Olmsted Brothers to create this vast house and gardens. Since 1968, the estate has operated as the Children's Education Center for AHRC Nassau. (PAT.)

WESTBURY HOUSE, 1904–1907 AND 1911. Now Old Westbury Gardens and open to the public, Westbury House was originally built as part of a marriage proposal by John S. "Jay" Phipps to Margarita C. Grace. Jay was one of the five children of Carnegie Steel partner Henry Phipps, and each of the children eventually lived in the Old Westbury vicinity. Jay and Margarita Phipps hired English designer George A. Crawley to create a home to raise their family. With the help of Crawley and landscape architect Jacques Gréber, Margarita designed the gardens to be reminiscent of her native England. Her favorite, the walled garden, was the inspiration for their daughter Peggy Phipps Boegner to create Old Westbury Gardens with the help of her brothers. (Above, PAT; below, PJM.)

Residence of J. S. Phipps, Westbury, N.Y.

SPRING HILL, 1900–1903. Jay Phipps's brother Henry Carnegie Phipps would buy this home, on the border of Roslyn and Old Westbury in 1906, just three years after its completion. The work of John Russell Pope, it was originally built for Wall Street broker William L. Stow. Located off Red Ground Road, the property is now a development bearing the estate's name. The house was demolished after Phipps's wife, Gladys, died in 1971. (PJM.)

THE CROSSROADS, 1919. A cousin of Margarita Phipps, William Russell Grace Jr. of W.R. Grace & Co. purchased a Quaker farmhouse in 1919 and hired James W. O'Connor to expand it. The rambling compound was designed to accommodate the family's sporting interests and included a wing containing a squash court, sunken tennis court, and an indoor riding school, or arena, which was later converted into a ballroom for large family events and daughter Patricia's wedding. It remains under private ownership. (T&C.)

KNOLE AND STABLE, 1903. Purchased in 1910 by Jay's sister Helen Phipps Martin, Knole was occupied by the Martin family for the next 91 years. Helen and her husband, Bradley Martin Jr., would make minor alterations to the home, but it remained largely unaltered from Carrère & Hastings's original 1903 design. Two of the largest changes were the additions of the library and two children's bedrooms, added above the living room to accommodate their twins, Esmond and Alastair. In the center of the 40,000-square-foot house is a massive, three-story oval rotunda, from which all the formal rooms radiate. It was the center of family activity, especially at Christmas, when it was decorated with a massive tree, and all the Phipps families would come to celebrate. Their son Esmond B. Martin, who lived there until his death in 2001, lovingly maintained the estate. The Martins and their four boys utilized the stable (below) and an indoor tennis court, which was added by Hastings in 1921. The stable and indoor tennis house were lost to fire before the Martins sold the estate. Subdivided by a developer, the house survives on a smaller lot. (Both, T&C.)

**BAGATELLE AND STABLES, 1911.** Renaissance Italy inspired Thomas Hastings when building for his own account. Hastings, of the noted firm Carrère & Hastings, was responsible for the New York Public Library and the Henry Clay Frick home (now the Frick Collection) in Manhattan. His favorite project was Knole, and it was said to be the home he would have designed for himself if he had the budget. That not being the case, Hastings modestly named his home Bagatelle, translated from Italian as "a thing of trifling importance." Not exactly that, it was, though, as Hastings described it in a 1914 interview for *Town & Country*: "Parva sed apta [small but fit]." Set on 15 acres in Old Westbury bordering H.C. Phipps, the house and stable are at opposing ends of a walled motor court, which serves as the main entrance to the house. The gardens were filled with architectural elements from Hastings's travels to Europe. Still owned privately, the house remains mostly intact on a smaller plot. (Both, ARCH.)

**WHITE EAGLE, 1916–1917.** The last of the Phipps sisters to purchase a house was Amy, who married Frederick Guest, a cousin of Winston Churchill. Built for Alfred I. du Pont by Carrère & Hastings, it was purchased by the Guests in 1921 for $470,000, a fraction of its $1.1 million construction cost. The house was renamed Templeton, and the Guests' son Winston and his wife, C.Z., resided there after Amy's death but sold the house to New York Institute of Technology in 1972 that has since operated it as a catering venue. (PJM.)

**ERCHLESS, 1931–1935.** Living in a Quaker farmhouse after he graduated from Yale in 1907, Howard Phipps, the youngest of the Phipps boys, remained a bachelor until 1931, when he married Harriet Dyer Price. Their new Old Westbury home was sited just north of the farmhouse, and construction was completed in 1935. Harriet took a strong interest in designing the house, working closely with their architect, Lewis Greenleaf Adams. It is the only Phipps house still owned by the original family. (LOC.)

**LONGFIELDS, 1910.** William B. and Edith Thompson commissioned Carrère & Hastings to design their country home in Old Westbury. The long drive, now divided by the Long Island Expressway, ran one mile up to the house. Unoccupied for several years, the estate was eventually sold to adjoining neighbor F. Ambrose Clark to enlarge Broad Hollow (page 41). The house was razed, and the property is now part of the State University of New York, Old Westbury. (LIS.)

**PELL RESIDENCE, 1920.** This large Colonial Revival located off Jericho Turnpike in Old Westbury was built for Howland Haggerty Pell Sr. A stockbroker, Pell was a descendent of Thomas Pell, who in 1654 purchased a swath of land from the Siwanoy Indians that is now Pelham and Pelham Manor. The house still exists today as a private residence. (PC.)

**HILLWOOD, THE GREAT HALL, 1921–1928.** Now Long Island University's C.W. Post Campus, Hillwood was constructed on the grounds of the William A. Prime estate. Marjorie Merriweather Post purchased the property in 1921 with her then husband, financier E.F. Hutton. She would hire Hart & Shape to build a rambling half-timbered Tudor on the Primes's foundation. The house was constantly evolving, and carpentry shops were set up on the property to create the woodwork. It took seven years to complete. The Great Hall saved from the old house reflected Hutton's sporting nature, with various mounts and antlers adding to the room's hunting-lodge feel. Post divorced Hutton in 1935, and he would purchase the house next door (page 62) to be close to his daughter. In 1951, Marjorie sold Hillwood to Long Island University for $200,000, which was less than half of what she paid for the land in 1921. (Both, HOW.)

**AUTUMN AT HILLWOOD, 1924.** General Foods and Post Cereal heiress Marjorie Merriweather Post is pictured with her one-year-old daughter Nedenia. This photograph was taken upon their return from Europe. The family would spend autumn at Hillwood before returning to New York City. During the winter, the family would go Palm Beach, first to her house on Golfview Road and then to Mar-A-Lago after its completion in 1927. Donald Trump now owns Mar-A-Lago as the Mar-a-Lago Club. Nedenia would go on to become well-known actress Dina Merrill. (A&D.)

**HUTFIELD, STAIR HALL, 1917.** E.F. Hutton purchased this home after his divorce from Marjorie Merriweather Post. At the age of 61, Hutton remarried in 1936 to the former Dorothy D. Metzger, who was 28 years old. Designed by John Russell Pope for J. Randolph Robinson, the house sat at the crest of a high rolling hill with sweeping views down a great lawn. The gardens ran just west of the house and meandered down the hill. The Huttons made minor renovations and renamed the house Hutfield. A swimming pool and cabana were added, backing the gardens. The home was decorated from top to bottom with sporting art, mounts, and equestrian paraphernalia, and an important work in the Huttons' collection was John Wootton's painting *The Warren Hill, Newmarket*. (Both, CL.)

**HUTFIELD STUDY AND STABLE, 1917.** The study at Hutfield featured works by John Ferneley, J.S. Herring, and, over the sofa, *Four Dogs* by J. Wheeler. Mementos and trophies of all kinds wrapped the room; even the "duck in flight" cartouche on the mantel added to the sporting theme. The house was decorated for comfort and livability, with overstuffed chairs and supple leather sofas along with Hutton's personal touches. Nestled into the hill northwest of the house, the shingle stable enclosed an open court, with the right wing containing room for staff. Shortly after her husband's death in 1962, Dorothy sold Hutfield to Long Island University. Still recognizable, the building has several extensions and has been covered in vinyl siding, changing its look slightly. (Both, CL.)

**RUMSEY RESIDENCE, 1910.** Polo player and sculptor Charles Cary Rumsey met his wife, Mary, while creating several works for her father, railroad magnate E.H. Harriman. These were to be installed at Arden House in what is now Harriman, New York. By 1910, the couple was married and ready to move into their home bordering Old Westbury and Brookville. Rumsey was killed in a car accident in 1922 near the couple's home. Mary would sell the house and build a new one at Sands Point (page 27). (PC.)

**OAK HILL, 1915.** The Meadowbrook Hunt is pictured in the court of Arthur Scott and Cynthia Roche Burden's Brookville residence. Arthur was head of Burden Iron Works of Troy, New York, and brother of James Burden of Woodside (page 95). The English Cynthia Roche Burden was a great aunt of Princess Diana of Wales. An active horseman, Arthur Burden died at the age of 42 in 1921. Cynthia Burden eventually remarried to become Mrs. Guy Fairfax Cary. (ARCH.)

**OAK HILL AND STAIR HALL, 1915.** Designed by noted architect John Rusell Pope, the house was situated on 75 acres and set in a wooded thicket of old fruit trees on the northeast corner of Cedar Swamp and Fruitledge Roads in Brookville. Appearing modest in size, it was an illusion of scale. The front door stood over nine feet tall, and the bricks, windows, and doors were all oversized. The main hall, as seen from the stairs, runs about 30 feet, and the walls are finished in a pale gray hard plaster to resemble highly polished stone. The elliptical staircase is set with iron spindles and a bronze railing. Cynthia Burden occupied the home, decorated like an English country house, for over 35 years, until she offered it for sale for $200,000 in 1949. Her daughter Eileen would marry publisher Walter Maynard and reside next door at Haut Bois. The house was demolished shortly after the sale. (Both, ARCH.)

**RYNWOOD AND DINING ROOM, 1927.** Sir Samuel A. Salvage, best known for developing rayon fabric, asked architect Roger H. Bullard to produce a home reminiscent of his native England. The result resembled the Cotswold cottages of Elizabethan England. He named the home for his wife, Mary Katherine, or "Ryn," and the wooded acres on which the house sits. Landscape architect Ellen Biddle Shipman laid out the gardens. Lady Salvage held onto the estate until 1947, when it then passed through a succession of owners, sitting empty for three years before hosting a designers' showcase in 1979. In 1980, wine importer Banfi Vintners purchased the estate as its world headquarters. After the company took possession in 1980, a restoration of the house and gardens ensued. Still prospering, it serves as an example of a successful adaptive reuse for an old estate. (Above, PJM; below, T&C.)

**RICHMOND HOUSE, LIVING HALL, 1928.** Bordering his sister Lady Katherine Salvage's home (page 66), L. Martin Richmond constructed a more modest estate on 15 acres. Pleased by his sister's home, Richmond retained Bullard and Shipman to design his house and garden. Instead of stone, Bullard utilized shingle, clapboard, and brick, giving the home its own personality. Surrounding the house, Shipman planned a natural, informal garden, taking advantage of the large oaks on the property and adding bits of color with dogwoods. The interiors were Early American in design, with the ceiling in the living hall held by exposed pine beams. In the 2000s, the house underwent massive renovations, and the exterior was covered entirely in brick. Only the living hall retains part of its original design. (Both, A&D.)

**BROADHOLLOW AND SUPERINTENDENT'S COTTAGE, 1926.** William T. Aldrich, an architect trained at the Massachusetts Institute of Technology, would design Broadhollow for his brother Winthrop A. Aldrich. Winthrop, quite distinguished in his own right, was founder of Chase National Bank, the US ambassador to the Court of St. James, and a noted philanthropist. Encompassing 106 acres off Cedar Swamp Road, a winding drive past a white shingle gatehouse led up a hill to the main house. Pictured is the back terrace, which overlooked a sweeping lawn. The estate contained a chicken house, vegetable garden, and greenhouse, which enabled the Aldriches to have fresh eggs, produce, and flowers. The superintendent's cottage, seen below, was six rooms attached to an eight-car, heated garage with a chauffeur's quarters above. In 1950, Aldrich sold the house to Alfred Gwynn Vanderbilt for $200,000. The house passed through two additional owners before the land was partially developed in the late 1980s and completed in the early 1990s. The house survives, but the outbuildings have been razed. (Both, PJM.)

**MICHAEL GAVIN FARM GROUP, 1928.**
In November 1906, Gertrude Hill, the daughter of railroad tycoon James J. Hill, married Michael Gavin, an attorney. In 1928, the couple commissioned John Russell Pope to design them a French-style manor house that would complement the chapel Gertrude Hill Gavin had purchased in France and incorporated into the house. The couple asked prominent farm-group architect Alfred E. Hopkins to design them a farm that would keep with the style of the main house. A couple of years after Michael Gavin's death in 1960, the main house was destroyed by fire. Miraculously, the chapel was not damaged, and was donated to Marquette University. Instead of rebuilding after the fire, the farm group pictured here was converted to the main house, and it survives in ruinous condition. (Both, H&G.)

**WELWYN, 1904–1916 AND 1920.** Welwyn, the home of Harold I. Pratt, was part of a large swath of land in Glen Cove purchased by his father, Charles Pratt, a partner at Standard Oil. The Pratt family land holdings collectively boasted over 1,200 acres. Nearly all of Charles's children would build estates around Glen Cove and be buried in the family mausoleum, which was designed by William B. Tubby and Tiffany Studios bordering their estates in Lattingtown. Babb, Cook & Welch completed the original house (above) in 1904. The shingle residence was replaced by an updated brick version by Delano & Aldrich in 1920 (below). The estate shared the family farm complex known as the Pratt Oval, a small part of which still exists as commercial space. (Both, MM.)

**WELWYN TENNIS COURT, 1920.** The 200-acre waterfront Welwyn was a lush preserve of native woodland and gardens of all varieties, which were laid out by James Greenleaf and, later, by the Olmsted Brothers. There were both indoor and outdoor tennis courts. A decorative trellis surrounded the outdoor court, while the indoor court was decorated in a nautical theme. After Mrs. Harold (Harriet Barnes) Pratt's death in 1969, the property became the Nassau County Welwyn Preserve, and today, the house is the Holocaust Memorial and Tolerance Center. (MM.)

**THE MANOR HOUSE, 1909–1915.** Harold's brother John Teele Pratt hired architect Charles Platt to complete his home. He and his wife, Ruth, had five children. Ruth, the former Ruth Sears Baker, was one of the first women elected to the US Congress. Their son John Teele Pratt Jr. built two houses bordering the property to the east, the earlier of which still stands. The Manor House operates today as a hotel and conference center. (PJM.)

HUMPHREYS/WOOLWORTH RESIDENCE, 1899–1902 AND WINFIELD, 1916–1920. Best known as Winfield, this was the home of five-and-dime store founder F.W. Woolworth. After a devastating fire in 1916 destroyed his Mediterranean-style home, which had been designed by C.P.H. Gilbert for Alexander C. Humphreys, Woolworth requested Gilbert to design a new fireproof residence. To meet his client's request, the new house would be built solidly of a pale pinkish marble. Two years after the house was completed, Woolworth died, and Winfield was sold fully furnished to the Reynolds family of Reynolds Wrap and Aluminum fortune. Of all the houses designed by Gilbert, only Winfield and a handful of his smaller projects remain standing. (Above, PJM; below, AR.)

**WINFIELD STAIRS AND GARDEN, 1916–1920.** This lavish showplace would be one of the most decadent houses on the North Shore. Not only was the building constructed of marble, but a good portion of its interiors were decorated with the expensive stone, including the entire entrance hall and staircase, which were rumored to have cost several million dollars. Upstairs, each bedroom was decorated in a different period or theme. There were rooms styled in themes such as Chinese Ming dynasty, Gothic, and Edwardian, and the master bedroom was modeled in a Napoleonic theme. After the Reynolds' tenure, the house was converted to the short-lived Grace Downs School. By 1976, the estate was converted back to a residence, and shortly after it was leased to the Pall Corporation. Since the early 2000s, it is again a private residence and backdrop for a number of Hollywood films, such as the 2011 HBO remake of *Mildred Pierce*. (Both, AR.)

**MATINECOCK POINT AND DAIRY, 1909–1913.** On East Island, off the shore of Glen Cove, was the house of financier J.P. Morgan Jr. When seen from the air, it is easy to see why the area is called Matinecock Point. To design his estate, Morgan approached architect Christopher Grant LaFarge (son of prominent artist John LaFarge), who had recently finished an addition to Pres. Theodore Roosevelt's Sagamore Hill. LaFarge would not only design the main house on the 140-acre island, but also a large farm complex, with a milk and dairyman's house (below), at a cost of $2.5 million. The house was full of nautically themed ornamentation, and the walled garden contained a marble fountain said to be a gift from the king of Italy. Partially developed in the 1950s, the main house remained a convent until it was put up for sale for $850,000, sold, and eventually demolished in 1980. The dairy complex and gardener's cottage remain as private residences. (Above, PJM; below, PFA.)

ROUND BUSH AND APPLE TREES, 1917–1918. J.P. Morgan Jr. purchased around 60 acres of land at the corner of Duck Pond and Piping Rock Roads. He then hired Roger Bullard to design houses as wedding presents for his daughter Francis Tracy Morgan and his son Junius S. Morgan. Each house sat on approximately 30 acres and, while similar in style, had very different floor plans. For Francis Tracy and her husband, Paul G. Pennoyer, Round Bush would be a home loved forever. The house would only change hands after her death (page 125). Junius would sell Apple Trees when West Island, which bordered his father's island, became available. There, he would again request the help of Bullard to design Salutations in 1930. Both of the J.S. Morgan houses survive. (Both, PFA.)

EAST GATES AND APPROACH TO ORMSTON HOUSE, 1912–1918. A self-made millionaire, John E. Aldred was the head of numerous rail, utility, and manufacturing companies, including the Gillette Safety Razor Company. The grounds of the estate were laid out first by landscape firm Olmsted Brothers, followed by architect Henry W. Rowe. Rowe designed the stables and the picturesque east and west gate lodges, with iron gates by Samuel Yellin. Last to be constructed was the massive Elizabethan-style stone house by Bertram G. Goodhue. The Olmsted Brothers would be on retainer for the next three decades, supervising and improving the grounds. Through a series of bad investments in Italy during World War II, Aldred lost his fortune and sold the home, which now operates as the St. Josaphat's Monastery. (Above, PAT; below, PJM.)

MEUDON AND VIEW FROM TERRACE, 1900. Born in San Francisco, prominent attorney William D. Guthrie spent his childhood in France, was educated in England, and would ultimately settle in Lattingtown at the turn of the 20th century and construct a tremendous limestone house high on a hill overlooking Long Island Sound. The gardens spread out over 300 acres and stretched from the back terrace down the hill all the way to the Sound, and at the shore was a wooden bath pavilion. To achieve an unobstructed view, Guthrie collaborated with his new neighbor, John E. Aldred, to purchase and bulldoze everything in their path, which totaled upwards of 60 homes and businesses that made up the village of Lattingtown. This collaboration essentially exterminated the business district of the small village. Guthrie would later serve as the village's first mayor in 1931. The C.P.H. Gilbert design was modeled after the great 16th-century palaces of France. Generous with his church, Guthrie donated the land across from Meudon in 1912 to form St. John's of Lattingtown and was active there until his death in 1935. Mrs. Guthrie (Ella E. Fuller) remained at Meudon for nearly two more decades. In 1956, the contents of the home were auctioned off, the house razed, and the property developed. Today, a number of the outbuildings have been converted into residences, and the old farm is still in operation as the Armstrong Dairy. (Above, PC; below, T&C.)

**A.C. Bedford Gates, 1900.** Still standing on Overlook Road in Lattingtown are the massive brick posts and iron gates from the home of Standard Oil chairman Alfred C. Bedford. The gates are also known as the entrance to the John W. Davis house, which was constructed at the turn of the century. Davis was a founding partner of Davis Polk Wardwell. In 1923, Bedford would sell his 60 acres in Lattingtown and move to Blythewood, a Georgian-style estate off Northern Boulevard in Muttontown. (PJM.)

**Reynold's Residence, 1919.** Deciding to build near his business associates and friends, Jackson E. Reynolds, president of the First National Bank, constructed his house in Lattingtown just a stone's throw away from his former bosses, George F. Baker and Francis L. Hine. Harrie T. Lindebergh's design for the house incorporated a striking spiderweb-themed iron front door. It remains private. (AR.)

**HOMEWOOD, 1924.** Edith Pratt, a daughter of Herbert L. Pratt, married Allan McLane Jr. at her parents' apartment at 1027 Fifth Avenue in November 1919. The firm of Carrère & Hastings was enlisted to design homes for both her and her sister Mrs. Lawrence Bell (Harriet) Van Ingen (page 22). McLane's Homewood and the Van Ingens' Preference both survive. (SPUR.)

**E.I. ELDREDGE RESIDENCE, 1920.** A stockbroker at Bull & Eldredge, Edward Irving Eldredge settled in Glen Cove near the home of his wife's (the former Althea Gibb) parents. Renovating a sizeable 1850s house, architect Howard Major stripped it of its earlier ornamentation, replacing it with a large two-story portico. The interiors were updated in the Greek Revival style as well. Today, the house remains standing with several modern extensions, but its large Ionic columns have been removed and replaced by steel beams. (CL.)

WOODFIELD AND OUTDOOR LIVING ROOM, 1910. Making his money as counsel for the railroad industry and later as president of E.H. Harriman, Robert S. Lovett asked Carrère & Hasting to build his Lattingtown home. The Lovetts had one son, Robert Abercrombie Lovett, who would build his own home in Locust Valley and go on to serve as the US secretary of defense under President Truman. Woodfields was sold to Trevor Diebold after Lovett's death in 1932 and razed by 1938. The gates survive as the entrance to a development off Bayville Road. (Both, BB.)

**MUNNYSUNK, 1911–1912.** Frank Bailey, founder of the Museum of the City of New York and developer of several major Brooklyn communities, settled in Lattingtown. Purchasing a modest farmhouse dating back to 1810, Bailey hired H. Craig Severance to remodel it and settled in by 1912. The Baileys had a good sense of humor and derived the name "Munnysunk" in honor of the high costs associated with the home. The property exists as the Bailey Arboretum. (CL.)

**PORTLEDGE, SOUTH GARDEN FRONT, 1910.** The country house of Charles A. Coffin, president and founder of General Electric, was positioned in a vast field bordered by deep woods. The family would gather to watch sunsets on the colonnade of the south garden. Portledge was one of three homes on the North Shore designed by New York architect Howard Greenley. All of Greenley's designs are still standing. Portledge is now a private school. (ARCH.)

**OAK POINT, 1903–1920 AND OAK POINT PLAYHOUSE, 1927–1928.**
Originally named Dunstable, the Bayville home of Winslow S. Pierce was renamed by the stylish Harrison and Mona Williams, who purchased the estate in 1920. Hidden behind a high brick wall and overlooking Long Island Sound, the 80-room brick house underwent a massive renovation with the help of Delano & Aldrich and Mr. Williams's utility company fortune. In 1929, he was said to have controlled one-fifth of the country's utilities. Mona Williams, the former Mrs. Harry Schlesinger, was considered one of the best-dressed women in the country; her style rivaled that of her peer C.Z. Guest. The Williamses divided their time between their homes at 1130 Fifth Avenue, Paris, Capri, Palm Beach, and Oak Point. Delano would return to the estate in 1927 to design a large indoor recreation house, complete with a series of lavish entertaining rooms. (Both, HOW.)

OAK POINT PLAYHOUSE, 1927–1928. This lavish structure was equipped like a fine hotel, and the Williamses spared no expense. In addition to the indoor tennis court and pool, the steel and brick building's most interesting space was a large living room in the Art Deco style. Like something out of Rockefeller Center, the room had a vaulted ceiling, striking murals painted on platinum leaf by Spanish artist José Maria Sert, and drapes consisting of hundreds of strands of silver beads. During World War II, the Williamses closed the main house and converted the playhouse into a more manageable dwelling by covering the indoor pool with parquet flooring and transforming the tennis court into a lush indoor garden complete with colorful tropical plants and birds. By the 1960s, both the house and playhouse were demolished, and the high brick wall that surrounded the estate was converted into the entrance to a development named for the estate. (Both, PAT.)

**New House, 1904.** In 1904, publishing giant Frank Nelson Doubleday asked John Petit of Kirby, Petit & Green to design him a home at Mill Neck. The shingle house underwent several alterations. It is seen here shortly before it burned in 1914. Two years later, architect Kenneth M. Murchison built a fireproof brick Tudor on the old foundation for Sen. William J. Tully. Tully was the father of Alice Tully, namesake of Lincoln Center's Alice Tully Hall. It still stands under private ownership. (CL.)

**Barberrys, 1916.** Nelson Doubleday, son of Frank Nelson Doubleday, worked with Locust Valley architect Harrie T. Lindeberg to create Barberry's at Mill Neck in 1916. Lindeberg called upon Oscar Bach to execute the ironwork at the main entrance, similar to the Lutz house (page 22) in Oyster Bay Cove. Expert in a variety of styles, Lindeberg would give Doubleday a house inspired by the Mediterranean. The house remains privately owned. (AR.)

GOOSE POINT, 1914. Olympic figure skater and clothier Irving Brokaw built his estate at the edge of series of ponds in Mill Neck. Executed with a signature Harrie T. Lindeberg undulating roofline, the house became a bit too small for Brokaw, and in 1926 he hired Walker & Gillette to create Frost Mill Lodge, a larger brick residence at the top of the hill overlooking the ponds. Both still survive. (PJM.)

THE CHIMNEYS, 1928. In 1928, Charles Porter Wilson, an executive at the Great Atlantic and Pacific Tea Company (A&P), commissioned Hart & Shape to build him and his family a house at Mill Neck. The resulting home was a spectacular half-timber and herringbone-brick residence considered by *Country Life* magazine to be "among the finest adaptations of Tudor-style in this country." It remains in pristine condition. (HOW.)

**OAK KNOLL, 1916–1918.** Oak Knoll was built for Bertram G. Work, president of B. F. Goodrich Co., and is located on a 13.5-acre plot in Mill Neck. Built at the top of hill, the Neoclassical Oak Knoll remains a favorite of many Delano & Aldrich fans. Delano created a three-part entrance. First visible from the road is a striking walled entrance court at the bottom of the hill; next, through the iron gates, the driveway winds up a steep incline of nearly 50 feet, opening at the final arrival court, which is paved in cobblestone. A reflecting pool and the house stand at opposing ends. The entrance, which is covered in pale cream stucco and trimmed in limestone, reflects the work of Andrea Palladio. The limestone crown reflects signs of the sea, with scallop shells, turtles, and other sea life along with ironwork by Samuel Yellin of Philadelphia. (PAT.)

**BREAKFAST ROOM AND PERGOLA AT OAK KNOLL, 1916–1918.** Extending from the northeast corner of the house, Delano placed the breakfast room to catch morning sun and views of Oyster Bay. The walls, painted with true frescoes by Gardner Hale, depict a fanciful, bird-filled paradise. The garden proved to be a challenge to place, since the land had a steep slope. Contained within a wall on three sides southwest of the house, the garden is linked to the house by a long pergola covered in wisteria and potted hydrangeas and open to a view of the bay. Privately owned, the house and gardens remain in perfect condition. (Both, PAT.)

**Margrove and Entrance Hall, 1930.** An article published in *Country Life* entitled "Margrove: an Aviator's Home" sums it up perfectly. Symbols of flight were incorporated throughout the house. Designed by its owner, noted engineer, airplane designer, and founder of the Loening Aeronautical Engineering Corp. Grover Loening, the home is located at the western end of Mill Neck. The exterior is free of ornament with the exception of a roof-deck railing with an open-wing motif. The front door, studded with chromium stars, suggests the night sky. The interior does not disappoint either, as the steel railing is cut into the pattern of gulls in flight, and canvases mounted to the gray walls depict Loening's own planes high in the clouds. The house remains private, but Loening's unique designs have been completely erased. (Both, CL.)

**La Selva Garden and Pool, 1915–1917.** With collaboration between Hunt & Hunt and the Olmsted Brothers, La Selva featured all the amenities of a vast 100-acre estate perfectly sited and scaled for 24 acres. Reminiscent of an old Northern Italian villa, its rough pebble-dash stucco walls and terra-cotta roof tiles glazed with hints of green to give the appearance of age. Its owner, businessman Henry Sanderson, used the house strictly in the summer, and within 10 years sold it to Frederick S. Wheeler of American Can Co. The Olmsted Brothers would advise and expand the gardens for over two decades, and their last major expansion was to create an oval swimming pool tucked in a secluded valley of flowering trees and shrubs. Serving the Catholic Church as St. Francis Retreat House from 1960 until 2001, today it remains intact and is privately owned. (Both, BR.)

COE HALL, 1919–1926. William Robertson and Mai Rogers Coe first purchased the James Byrne house in 1913. Completed in 1906 by Grosvenor Atterbury, the estate encompassed over 400 acres. During renovations, the house was lost to a fire in 1918, and the Coes would ask the firm Walker & Gillette to construct a new home reminiscent of Mr. Coe's native England. Built from a warm gray Indiana limestone, the house appeared to be an Elizabethan manor that had evolved over generations. (PJM.)

BREAKFAST ROOM AT COE HALL, 1920. The breakfast room at Coe Hall, affectionately called the "Buffalo room," was the work of artist Robert Winthrop Chanler and reflects the Coe's interests in the American Midwest. Chanler, great-grandson of William Backhouse Astor Sr., was a popular society painter known for his screens and murals, and his Long Island clients included Gertrude Whitney (page 47) and Mary Rumsey (pages 27 and 64.) Chanler would return a year later to decorate Mrs. Coe's bedroom. (PAT.)

**COE HALL, ITALIAN GARDENS, 1918–1929.** With the good bones for a garden surviving from the Byrneses' occupation of the property, the Coes went to work adding to the gardens. Guy Lowell, Andrew Robeson Sargent, and ultimately the Olmsted Brothers would take charge of the grounds. The Italian gardens seen here were originally the tennis court when the Coe family purchased the property. Sargent, who died before the work finished, had started the conversion, but the Olmsted Brothers would see them through completion. Open to the public, the house and grounds exist as the Planting Fields Arboretum and are run by New York State and the Planting Fields Foundation. (Right, PAT; below, CL.)

**GRAY HORSE FARM AND STABLE, 1924.** True equestrians Geraldyn and Katherine Redmond's Upper Brookville home was literally centered around horses. They were active in racing in the United States and France and were riders with the Meadowbrook Hunt. The house and stable adjoined to form a large open court. The work of architect James W. O'Connor and landscape architect Robert Ludlow Fowler, the house was sited in what was an open field, so Fowler brought in mature boxwood and trees to add age to the landscape. Constructed of whitewashed brick with greenish-blue shutters, the garden front opened up to a grass and stone terrace overlooking a vast lawn. The stalls were lined with ash, and the timber was hand hewn to give a rustic look, as if they had been there for years. Equally old, but added to the estate by a later owner, the gates to J.P. Morgan's Matinecock Point (page 74), mark the entrance. (Above, PJM; below, PC.)

**GRAY HORSE FARM, HALL AND DINING ROOM, 1924.** The interior of the house reflected the family's sporting interests, with silver trophies and spoils of their stable sprinkled throughout. The hall was papered in a hunting scene by Zuber and furnished with a mixture of French and American antiques. Incorporated into one wall of the dining room was paneling and a fireplace taken from an 18th-century farmhouse in Poughkeepsie. The remainder of the room was finished with old, scenic French paper. Several years after Redmond's death in 1930 at the age of 36, the property was sold to a series of horsemen, including polo player Stephen "Laddie" Sanford. Although now subdivided, the house still sits in a country landscape, and its paddocks are still filled with horses. (Both, CL.)

**Harvey S. Ladew Residence, 1916.** Harvey S. Ladew commissioned James W. O'Connor to design him a country house at Upper Brookville so that he could enjoy foxhunting with the Meadowbrook Hunt. From the exterior, it appears that O'Connor designed a straightforward Dutch Colonial with a sleeping porch and glass-enclosed breakfast room; however, the interiors of the house were Jacobean in their architectural details and furnishings. The house remains privately owned. (H&G.)

**Muttontown Meadows, 1903.** In 1903, New York attorney Bronson Winthrop purchased 450 acres at Muttontown and commissioned Delano & Aldrich to build him a retreat. The architects took inspiration from Mount Vernon when designing the exterior facade; however, the interiors were decidedly French. In time, Bronson Winthrop asked the architects to build him a different house on his property, and gave this house to his brother Egerton. Renamed Nassau Hall, it is now part of the Muttontown Preserve. (PAT.)

MUTTONTOWN CORNERS, 1914–1915. Architect William Adams Delano of Delano & Aldrich built his own country place, Muttontown Corners, on 10 acres on the corner of the 450-acre Bronson Winthrop estate (page 94). Thriving, the firm's roster had close to 40 North Shore houses to its credit. Delano's house is privately owned, but the outbuildings exist as administration offices for the Long Island Lutheran School, which occupies Highpool, the former W. Deering Howe estate across the road. (AR.)

WOODSIDE, 1916–1918. During the international polo match of 1924 at Meadowbrook, the Prince of Wales was welcomed at Woodside, the home of James A. Burden. Receiving accolades for its design, it is considered one of Delano & Aldrich's finest homes. Surrounded by gardens laid out by the Olmsted Brothers, the grounds often played host to the Meadowbrook Hunt and horse shows. Later, it was converted to the Woodcrest Country Club, and after financial turmoil, it was auctioned off for $19 million in 2010. The new owner's intentions for the property remain unknown. (CL.)

**BRIDGE NEAR YANGTZE RIVER, 1921 AND MOAT BRIDGE AT CHELSEA, EARLY 1930S.** Alexandra Moore took the above photograph, one of dozens delivered to her architect, William Delano, in China on her honeymoon trip to Europe and Asia. The Muttontown home was complete with a moat on two sides, the gardens and predominantly French-style home a successful blend of the architecture of Europe and Asia. The moon gate and bridge (pictured) were copied at Chelsea to connect the rear terrace to the garden. The rear terrace became the center of social and family activity, and the bridge was a popular spot for family photographs. The Moore's three children seen on the bridge are, from left to right, Alfred, Linda, and Alexander (Both, PJM.)

CHELSEA, 1923–1924 AND MOORE FAMILY, EARLY 1930S. Chelsea was constructed between 1923 and 1924 for Benjamin and Alexandra Moore. Benjamin Moore was an attorney, with no relation to the paint company bearing the same name. The estate was named for Chelsea, England, from which their family emigrated in 1750, and area on the west side of Manhattan, which was the original family farm, also still known as Chelsea. The Moores' Sunday lunch was a ritual well-liked by family and friends and usually consisted of about 20 guests. In good weather, the Moores' butler, Ogilvie, would set up the buffet under the large apple tree on the terrace. Here, with arms extended, are the Moores' guests, who are enjoying one of those lunches. For the children, the moat doubled as a place to cool off in the summer. Alexander and Alfred are captured here enjoying a swim with the family dogs. Alexandra Moore lived at Chelsea until her death in 1983. She willed the estate to Nassau County as part of the Muttontown Preserve. (Both, PJM.)

**CHARLTON HALL AND STAIRS, 1916–1917.** The site of the first village elections, the Muttontown home of sportsman David Dows took full advantage of the talents of noted Philadelphia architect Horace Trumbauer. Trumbauer filled the home, modeled after England's Groombridge Place, with a number of antique English mantels and a staircase, which, according to *Town and Country* magazine, belonged to the Duke of Cumberland. The house has grand-scale entertaining rooms that would be in line with a house double the size. The living room is large enough to construct two Levitt houses inside of it. The stair hall, like the lobby of a hotel, was the center of family and social activity. Utilizing the terrace, all the rooms on the first floor could serve as one large party space of nearly 5,000 square feet. Later residents would include Wolocott Blair, Watson K. Blair, and his stepdaughter, fashion icon Mary McFadden. Charlton Hall still remains in private hands with minimal alterations. (Both, T&C.)

**CA VA, 1929–1930.** This was the second North Shore home built by Lehman Brothers broker Carroll B. Alker. He sold his first on Cedar Swamp Road in Old Brookville shortly after its completion in 1924. Locust Valley architect Bradley Delehanty received the commission for this home. French with a modern flair, the Alker house was like something out of a storybook. The front courtyard overlooked a small pond, while the rear focused on a terraced garden punctuated by a pool and garden folly. The interiors also reflected traditional French styles with a hint of 1930s Art Deco. Later, Esmond Bradley Martin lived in the house until he moved his family home back to Knole (page 56). After Martin sold the property, the house and gatehouse on Brookville Road became part of a small subdivision. (Both, T&C.)

**GATE LODGE AND TERRACE AT WINDFALL, 1927–1930.** The Francis T. Nichols house is the only known North Shore home designed by Howard & Frenaye. The gate lodge and garage complex reflect the French architecture, which would provide influence for the main house. The Nichols lived in the gate lodge during the construction of the main house, which was completed three years later. Pictured below is a view from the terrace looking toward the breakfast-room turret. Constructed of brick and half-timbering, the house has Frenaye's Ludovici tile roof and fanciful carved woodland creatures as ornamentation. The two structures remain private homes. (Both, CL.)

KNOLLWOOD, 1906–1911. Photographed shortly after landscape architect Ferruccio Vitale transformed the 300-acre farmland into a series of parklike vistas for stockbroker Charles I. Hudson, the limestone house, designed by Hiss & Weekes, is best known for an owner who never even lived there, the exiled King Zog of Albania. Left empty by Zog, the house was ransacked by curious visitors, effectively forcing demolition. Today, the grounds are part of the Muttontown Preserve, and the gates stand as a reminder off Route 106. (HB.)

KIRBY HILL, 1904. In 1904, Joseph Sampson Stevens, an avid sportsman and a member of Theodore Roosevelt's Rough Riders, commissioned Warren & Wetmore to construct his house and stable at Muttontown. Owned by the family for nearly 100 years, the 146-acre property was sold in 2000 for a record $21 million by Byam Stevens, the former mayor of the village. The main house is now in the center of a gated community with 86 homes, called Stone Hill at Muttontown. (PJM.)

**FRANK C.B. PAGE RESIDENCE FRONT AND REAR FACADES, 1916–1920.** The brick Georgian home of Frank C. Bauman Page, executive of the E.W. Bliss Company, was conceived in late 1916 when Page purchased the adjoining Seaman and Mitchell farms, totaling 66 acres. Located in what was Oyster Bay, it is now part of Upper Brookville. The tiny village might not have been Upper Brookville without resident Mrs. Charles Oliver (Hope Goddard) Iselin, who is said to have caused quite a fuss when she heard its suggested name of Lower Brookville. She refused to live anywhere called "lower," so the residents settled on Upper Brookville in 1932. Little & Brown designed the main house, semicircular stable, and garage complex. The house consisted of 27 rooms and 11 baths on three floors. (Both, PJM.)

ENTRANCE HALL AND INDOOR POOL AT PAGE RESIDENCE, 1916–1920. Pictured are the entrance hall and indoor swimming pool as they appeared when it was owned by New York's 43rd governor, Nathan L. Miller. While the country house of Governor Miller, it was the scene of lavish parties hosted by Miller's son-in-law, airline executive Alvin P. Adams. Adams is cited in his *New York Times* obituary as a man "who came of age in the Roaring Twenties and never outgrew the roar." The parties stopped shortly before Miller's death in 1953, when the house was sold to the Soviet Mission for use as a diplomatic facility. The Russian Federation continues to own it today. (Both, PJM.)

FARLANDS AND FARM GROUP, 1917. The Guernsey Curran residence was completed in December 1917. The main house was designed by Guy Lowell and surrounded by formal gardens and a large circular amphitheater. The estate, dubbed Farlands, stretched out over 90 acres in Upper Brookville and featured an indoor tennis and pool house connected to the main house via an underground tunnel. The farm group was a signature Alfred E. Hopkins design. Today, the gatehouse, indoor tennis house, and farm group are all that survive. In 2005, a renovation to bring the Hopkins farm group closer to its original design began. The aluminum siding was removed, revealing the original clapboard and trim. The barn doors and windows were re-milled, and the cupola, silo, and weathervane restored. Its new owners are proud to have a piece of Farlands history. (Both, PJM.)

**FRAMEWOOD AND LIVING ROOM, 1914–1916.** Hoppin & Koen sited Framewood on a high, flat promontory to take advantage of the distant water views of Oyster Bay, making it one of the most peaceful places in Upper Brookville. Sterling Postley, lead counsel for the Singer Sewing Machine Co., purchased the land known as the Sammis estate in late 1914. The 19,000-square-foot home was set on 81 acres. Postley imported a number of paneled rooms from Europe, including an 18th-century Dutch breakfast room painted with hunting scenes. The most arresting features of the living room are the Italian carved wood columns that mark the entrance to the room from the main hall. The house and outbuildings still stand. (Both, ARCH.)

GATES AND REAR FACADE TO OLDFIELDS, 1934. Hidden at the end of a mile-long driveway off Northern Boulevard in Muttontown, Oldfields is best known as the residence of Louis Jacques and Consuelo Balsan, formerly Consuelo Vanderbilt, Duchess of Marlborough. The gates pictured mark the entrance to the motor court. Completed in 1934 for George Backer, it was constructed of hand-molded brick to the specifications of Treanor & Fatio. Backer's tenure was short-lived, and the Balsans acquired it in 1939. The Pine Hollow Country Club has called it home since 1955. It remains intact with several extensions. (Both, PGC.)

**MALLOW, 1918.** A favorite home of designers Ruby Ross Wood and Billy Baldwin, the house was decorated entirely by the owner, Mrs. Walter (Mildred Williams) Farwell. Matinecock resident William Welles Bosworth modeled the house in the English style and incorporated an 18th-century English staircase from the home of Lord Lytton into it. Pictured is the Farwells' 1928 Christmas card, given to the author by the chauffeur's daughter Lillian Hicks. The home has operated as East Woods School in Oyster Bay Cove since 1946. (PJM.)

"MALLOW"
Residence of Mr. Walter Farwell
Syosset, L. I.

**ONTARE, 1910.** Banker James A. Blair's Ontare was designed by Carrère & Hastings and completed in 1910. Located in Oyster Bay Cove, the estate encompassed a sizable swath of land between Cove and Sandy Hill Roads. Large in scale, the residence was approximately 25,000 square feet. Rather than being torn down when the property was developed, the home was divided in two. Separated by a common wall, the dwellings successfully remain separate but united. (ARCH.)

**WOODWARD PLAYHOUSE, 1928.** Originally part of Sunken Orchards, the recreational house of Charles E. F. McCann, set on approximately 40 acres, was sold to Ann and William Woodward Jr. as a residence in the early 1950s. Architect James W. O'Connor equipped the indoor tennis house with a number of guest and formal entertaining rooms. In 1955, the Oyster Bay couple made headlines when Mrs. Woodward, claiming to have mistaken him for a burglar, shot and killed her husband in the house at close range. She was exonerated at trial. (H&G.)

**WHITE EAGLE, 1929.** Beverly and Julia de Forest Duer hired Delano & Aldrich to design their house on the northwest corner of her parents' Laurel Hollow estate. As the house was under construction right before the stock market crash of 1929, midway through Beverly sent the following message to landscape architects Olmsted Brothers: "In light of what happened on Thursday (day of the crash) please cease all work at Laurel Hollow." The Duers eventually finished the work, and the house remains privately owned. (SPLIA.)

**ENTRANCE TO WOODLANDS, 1912–1915 AND BREAKFAST ROOM, 1931.** The Victor A. Morawetz house was another Delano & Aldrich design. The estate was complete with a working farm of horses, sheep, cattle, turkeys, and chickens. In 1928, Andrew Mellon gave it as a wedding present to his daughter Ailsa Mellon Bruce, who redecorated the house numerous times. The Schmitt Brothers decorated the sunroom, seen here, with murals by Victor White. At the time of her death in 1969, Ailsa Mellon Bruce was worth over $500,000,000, making her one of the wealthiest women in the United States. She was extremely charitable, and a number of foundations carry on her legacy. The Woodlands was given to the town of Oyster Bay, and today it is the Town of Oyster Bay Golf Course. The house serves as a restaurant and catering facility. It was expanded in the early 2000s, and only the front facade and several rooms on the first floor are recognizable. (Right, PAT; below, T&C.)

**Ogden Mills Residence, 1915.** In 1915, Ogden Mills commissioned architect John Russell Pope to design a home for him at Woodbury bordering H.R. Winthrop. Once the home was completed, over 1,000 mature trees were transplanted onto the property maintained by 15 gardeners. In 1937, the former secretary of the treasury under Hoover died, leaving an estate, which was worth over $9 million, to his wife, Dorothy, who in 1946 rented the house to Andrei Gromyko, the Soviet delegate to the United Nations Security Council. Mills would also commission Pope to design a smaller house for his daughter, which remains private. Ogden Mills's home is now gone, but several outbuildings and a brick wall along Jericho Turnpike stand as reminders. (PJM.)

**East Woods, 1910.** After a lengthy courtship, investment banker Henry Rogers Winthrop wed Alice Woodward Babcock. The couple married at the Stow residence (Spring Hill, page 55) in Roslyn, which the bride's parents were renting for the season in 1905 before it was sold to H.C. Phipps. The newlyweds engaged the firm d'Hauteville and Cooper to design a house on 400 acres at Woodbury. The house was lost to fire, but the gate survives on Juneau Boulevard. (PJM.)

**GOODWIN PLACE AND POOL, 1916–1917.** For his own residence, architect Philip Goodwin purchased a 35-acre farm bordering Woodbury Road, just south of Jericho Turnpike, from William B. Codling for $35,000. His land holdings would eventually grow to 196 acres. Taking down the 1738 farmhouse, Goodwin gave a room to the American Wing at the Metropolitan Museum of Art and incorporated the old beams from its barn into his living room ceiling and new farm complex. Strategically placed on the side of a hill, the house had three levels. The master bedroom, living room, and library were on the entry level. The dining room was placed one flight down and opened to a stone terrace and garden. Beyond the terrace, a swimming pool was surrounded by a wall and bathing pavilion. The house burned in 1975, and the site is now a housing development. (Above, CL; right, PJM.)

**OHEKA, 1914–1917.** Delano & Aldrich's largest private commission was the 108-room, château-inspired Oheka, built for financier Otto H. Kahn. It was upon completion, and remains today, the second-largest private house in the United States, complete with a private 18-hole golf course. The project was so massive, Kahn required a small army of workers to construct the estate. Having lost his house in New Jersey to fire, Kahn insisted Oheka be completely fireproof. His wife, Addie, sold Oheka in 1939, and it was renamed Sanita by the New York Department of Sanitation, which planned to use the house as a weekend retreat for its workers. Not properly zoned for Sanita, the dream was short-lived, and it became Eastern Military Academy until 1978. After the school left, it sat empty, was vandalized, and fires started in the ballroom; however, the fireproof house was only damaged and not destroyed. In 1984, Gary Melius purchased it and has brought the shell back to life, restoring it further each year. It operates as a historic hotel and wedding venue. The golf course is now the Cold Spring Hills Country Club, with the massive French-style stable as the clubhouse. (PJM.)

**LITTLE IPSWICH, 1927–1928.** One of Delano's favorite commissions belonged to his friend and noted interior designer Ruby Ross and her second husband, stockbroker Chalmers Wood. The house was named for Mr. Wood's childhood home of Ipswich, Massachusetts, and set on 43 acres in Woodbury. Little Ipswich maintained simple lines, refined classical details, and was described by one writer from *Architectural Digest* as "gemlike." Reported to be Delano's ideal country home, Little Ipswich was used as the background for his own portrait by Bernard Boutet de Monvel. Sold to Count Uzielli after Ruby Ross Wood's death in 1950, the home was razed in 1995 to make way for a modern development called Peromi Estates. (PC.)

**GLENMORA, 1930–1931.** The Cold Spring Harbor home of Linzee and Dorothea Blagden sits at the end of a long, wooded drive. The entrance hall with a spiral staircase leads up to the piano nobile with a large gallery hall. Off the gallery, the living room opens to a grass allée and a series of woodland gardens. Glenmora is located just a few minutes from its architect Frederick R. King's own home in Woodbury. Both houses are still privately owned. (GOTT.)

**DOUGLAS M. MOFFAT RESIDENCE, 1931.** The Moffat residence was part of a colony of manageable estates constructed on the Woodbury/Cold Spring Harbor border, which ran alongside the Bateson and Noyes residences. Noel and Miller designed this French-style house for Douglas M. Moffat and his wife, Gertrude. A partner at Cravath, Swaine & Moore during the Eisenhower administration, Moffat was appointed ambassador to Australia, where he ultimately passed away at age 74. The house still stands today. (CL.)

**LULWORTH, 1912–1914.** Daughter of Louis Comfort Tiffany of Tiffany Studios and granddaughter of Charles L. Tiffany of Tiffany & Co., Julia de Forest Tiffany would move to Lulworth with her second husband, Francis Minot Weld. Designed by Charles Platt with gardens by Olmsted Brothers, Ellen Shipman, and Platt, the house had been completed for Weld 15 years earlier. The Lloyd Harbor home survives on a smaller plot. (ARCH.)

ROSEMARY FARM, 1902–1908 AND AMPHITHEATER, 1912. Roland Ray Conklin made his money through several mortgage trusts and investments in Cuban banking and sugar. Purchasing the property in 1902, the Conklins lived in an enlarged farmhouse they renovated with the help of Philadelphia architect Wilson Eyre. A year later, Eyre would return to design the house pictured here. In 1912, an open-air theater inspired by ancient amphitheaters was constructed just below the main house and nestled into a hill overlooking Long Island Sound. Laid out by the Olmsted Brothers, the stage was actually an island separated from the audience by a water-filled, lagoon-like moat. In 1924, the Conklins left Rosemary Farm, selling it for $400,000. A seminary was built on the south end of the property, and the open-air theater was reclaimed by nature until the mid-1980s, when it was reopened for a single charity concert. Left empty, the house burned to the ground in 1990, and Conklin's amphitheater was left to nature once again. (Both, PC.)

**BURRWOOD AND ENTRANCE HALL, 1898.** Standard Oil's Walter B. Jennings's estate, dubbed Burrwood, spread out over 400 acres stretching from West Neck Road to Cold Spring Harbor. Carrère & Hastings's house design was an efficient use of the property's steep bluffs; the Neoclassic Georgian perched at the top afforded views across the harbor to Louis Comfort Tiffany's Laurelton Hall. One of the Olmsted Brothers first projects, the extensive grounds were developed over Jennings's 50-year tenure. Like a small village, the estate had 17 buildings and dwellings, and according to a 1938 insurance appraisal, had a replacement cost of nearly $350,000, staggering when the cost of an average new home that year was $3,900. The house alone stood over four stories, consisted of 50 rooms, and the entrance hall ran the full depth of the house, with a bay of French doors opening to a large terrace. The home was redecorated several times, and the photograph below reflects the Jennings' last remodel. (Both, PJM.)

**DARK HOLLOW AND ROTUNDA, 1930–1931.** The summerhouse of Oliver Burr Jennings was a gift from his father. Associate architects Mott B. Schmidt and Mogens Tvede were hired to design the house, which was located at the northwest corner of Burrwood. Teaming up several times, Schmidt, an American, and Tvede, a Dane, produced Dark Hollow in a style critics called "Neo-Palladian." Seen here from the Cold Spring Harbor side, the house was focused on a tremendous living room that occupied its entire center. Through the 20-foot-tall arched Palladian doorway, the ceiling inside the living room mimicked a barrel vault but soared even taller. The rotunda, as seen from the doorway to the living room, rose two stories, and the star pattern of the light fixture is repeated in a large skylight and on the terrazzo floor. Occupied until 2010, the home was left to vandals by new owners, who razed it in January 2012. (Both, H&G.)

117

**PANFIELD AND STAIR HALL, 1915.**
In 1915, prominent New York attorney Albert Goods Milbank engaged architect John Mead Hollows of Howells & Stokes to design a weekend retreat at Lloyd Harbor. Set on approximately 300 acres, the house commanded sweeping views of Huntington Harbor, the Lloyd Harbor lighthouse, and Long Island Sound. Passing the twin gate lodges, stables, and garages, the driveway runs a straight course to the front door. The house, faced in sand-colored stucco, was modeled after the pre-Elizabethan manor Compton Wynyates in Warwickshire, England. Paneled in oak and paved in a light brown tile, the stair hall reflects the later Jacobean style under the reign of James I. Concerned about overdevelopment, Milbank spearheaded the movement to incorporate Lloyd Harbor in 1926 and served as its first mayor. Panfield is still standing, though houses now line its 660-foot driveway. (Both, ARCH.)

**CRARY HOUSE AND LIVING ROOM, 1929.** Having family on Duck Island, Miner D. and Edith I. Crary would visit the hourglass-shaped island during the summer in the early 1920s. By 1929, the Crarys had purchased 22 acres, which consisted of the southwestern end of the hourglass. Architect Frederick L. Ackerman perched their new house on the highest bluff to afford 360-degree views of Northport Bay and the Sound. Following a so-called butterfly layout, wings extend from the central tower at a slight angle to take advantage of the view. Ackerman ordered the entire house, even the roof, be cloaked in hand-split Louisiana cypress to protect it from rot. The interiors were an eclectic mix of English and vernacular country styles. The overall feeling is harmonious and warm. Kept in the family for three generations, it was listed for sale in 2011. (Both, HOW.)

# Locust Valley Estate

20 acres—1100 feet of shore frontage. Land planted
with trees and shrubbery. High elevation commanding
an unobstructed view of the Sound.

House of stone and modern in every respect. Fireproof.
8 master bedrooms. 8 baths. 7 servant rooms. Stables
and 6-car garage with living quarters above.

Well built breakwater extends into the Sound forming
an excellent yacht basin and dock.

## Hamilton, Iselin & Co.

385 MADISON AVE.    *Murray Hill 7660*

Sole Agents—Brokers Protected

**COUNTRY ESTATES**
*Offered for Sale by Prince & Ripley, Inc and associated agents*

### DELIGHTFUL WATERFRONT ESTATE
Huntington, Long Island

A fine 22 acre estate and Colonial residence in the exclusive North Shore section—
the center of many fine suburban properties. About 1000 feet waterfront on Huntington Harbor. Residence; brick and frame construction. 20 rooms, with delightful oak
paneled living and dining rooms; 6 master bedrooms; 3 baths; 5 servants' bedrooms
and bath; Boynton steam heating, Richardson water heater. Garage, 2 cars, 4 rooms
and bath above; gardener's cottage, 4 rooms and bath; large barn and vegetable
storehouse; dock, bathhouse, bathing beach.

Descriptive and illustrated sheet No. 1338 upon request

*Local Prince & Ripley Agent*

**WM. E. GORMLEY, INC.**

HOTEL HUNTINGTON, HUNTINGTON, L. I.

*Huntington 2750*

CALLENDAR HOUSE FOR SALE, 1926 AND HUNTINGTON ESTATE AD, 1923. Even in the 1920s, houses were changing hands. Above, the Peter Winchester Rouss estate in Bayville is listed for sale; today, it is a nursing home. Another ad is for a 1900 Colonial Revival, known as the Henry Gilsey house, which borders the George Mckesson Brown estate (now Coindre Hall Park) on West Shore Road and is still privately owned. Many of these homes were often offered for a fraction of their original costs; Evelyn Marshall Field's Easton in Muttontown, costing an estimated $2.5 million to construct in 1931, sold for under $200,000 in 1951. Rather than see their homes developed, some residents donated them to charitable causes or public use. That was the case with Falaise (page 29), donated by Guggenheim to Nassau County and now open as part of the Sands Point Preserve, and the Vanderbilt house Eagle's Nest, now the Suffolk County Vanderbilt Museum. (Both, PJM.)

# *Three*

# CHANGING TIMES
# TO PRESENT

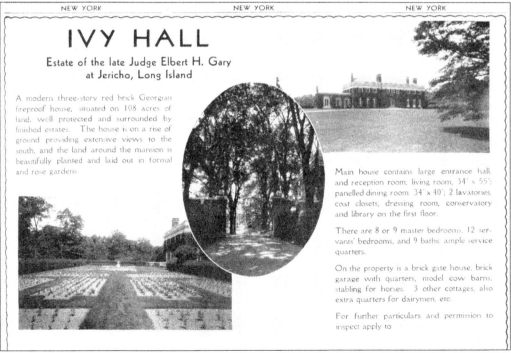

## IVY HALL

### Estate of the late Judge Elbert H. Gary
### at Jericho, Long Island

A modern three-story red brick Georgian fireproof house, situated on 108 acres of land, well protected and surrounded by finished estates. The house is on a rise of ground providing extensive views to the south, and the land around the mansion is beautifully planted and laid out in formal and rose gardens

Main house contains large entrance hall, and reception room; living room, 34' x 55'; panelled dining room, 34' x 40'; 2 lavatories, coat closets, dressing room, conservatory and library on the first floor.

There are 8 or 9 master bedrooms, 12 servants' bedrooms, and 9 baths; ample service quarters.

On the property is a brick gate house, brick garage with quarters, model cow barns, stabling for horses. 3 other cottages, also extra quarters for dairymen, etc.

For further particulars and permission to inspect apply to

IVY HALL OFFERING, 1930. Built by attorney Ralph J. Preston by the New York firm Warren & Wetmore, Ivy Hall was located off Jericho Turnpike in Jericho, now Muttontown. Judge Elbert Henry Gary, a US Steel founder and namesake of Gary, Indiana, occupied the house in the 1920s, but after the death of his wife, Emma, the contents sold at auction in 1935. The house was razed in 1950. Today, the gate lodge and a garage survive at private residences. (PJM.)

THE MONASTERY, 1925. Pictured above is an ad offering the perplexing dwelling of Juliana Armour Ferguson, heiress to the Armour meatpacking company. Christened the Monastery in 1911, it took three years to construct and was the work of Allen W. Jackson. Mrs. Ferguson's world revolved around children, as she had seven of her own, and she strangely had the floors paved with children's tombstones dating back three centuries. When Juliana lost her battle to cancer in 1921, her children sold the house. In 1964, the county seized the 14-acre waterfront estate for back taxes in excess of $100,000. It fell into ruin and was soon vandalized. Lost to the wrecking ball in 1970, the house did not fall quickly. Its concrete walls were over four feet thick, and its footings were 4-by-14 feet. The monumental task nearly bankrupted the project, and some of the footings and foundation remain clinging to the hill. The gatehouse is now a private home, and some of the garden walls stand today as reminders of Juliana Ferguson's castle. (Above, PJM; below, HH.)

BURRWOOD DEMOLITION, 1993. In the fall of 1949, a two-day auction ensued, and Park-Bernet sold off the contents of the estate. As the Industrial Home for the Blind, Burrwood remained trapped in time until it was sold to a developer in the early 1990s. Razed in 1993 and featured in all the local papers, it was not a popular decision made by the developer. Seen here carved into the Carrara marble above the front door is *Welcome to Burrwood*, which served as an eerie reminder and no longer as a greeting to those visiting the home. Still intact during demolition, the built-in drawers of the Jennings' map room are visible in the image below. Though the estate has been nearly erased, several outbuildings survive as private homes; part of the farm complex serves the community as Village Hall for Lloyd Harbor, and a small portion of the gardens remain. (Both, PC.)

**FLORA WHITNEY HOUSE DEMOLITION, 2001.** Sold by New York Institute of Technology in 1999 for approximately $10 million and sitting on 113 acres, the 1924 Delano & Aldrich house was replaced by an even larger home, rivaling the construction of the 1920s. The older home was sold for salvage, and many of its architectural elements were removed from the house before it was razed. Other homes lost about this time include the Livingston estate in Lloyd Harbor; the Hogan estate, formerly Camp Marshall Field, on Eatons Neck; the Dunbar Bostwick/Eben Pyne house in Old Westbury; Little Ipswich in Woodbury; the Cass Canfield house in Woodbury; the George Baker house on Centre Island; the John Teele Pratt Jr. house in Lattingtown; and the Wadsworth house in Muttontown. With several old homes lost each year, the history and style that make Long Island unique fade as well. (Both, WD.)

ROUND BUSH DEMOLITION, 1993. The family took this photograph during the last days of Round Bush (page 75), after the death of their mother, Frances Tracy Pennoyer. The ever-increasing property taxes reached $61,000 in 1989 and proved to be too much for the family. They were faced with the tough decision to sell the family home in Matinecock they so loved. Now, the gatehouse on Duck Pond Road marks the entrance to a development. (PPFA.)

VON STADE RUIN, 2005. This Old Westbury estate was a thriving horse farm for over 75 years and once part of baked goods giant William Entenmann's Timber Point Farm. Increased taxes and changing zoning laws in the late 1980s and 1990s threatened local horse farms, and many smaller stables were forced to close. Left for ruin by its new owners after demolition permits were denied in the 1990s, the house sat empty and decaying until February 2012, when it was purchased and razed to make way for a housing development. (PJM.)

**KILUNA FARM PLAYHOUSE, 1996.** Pictured is a view from the lounge of the indoor tennis court built for publisher Ralph Pulitzer by James W. O'Connor. The estate was later the 80-acre weekend home of William S. and Barbara "Babe" Paley from 1964 until 1986. Purchased by a developer, it sat empty for over a decade, during which the main house by Walker & Gillette was lost to fire. In 1997, the tennis house was demolished, and the property was developed with 87 homes. (PJM.)

**KEEWAYDIN'S LAST DAYS, 2011.** A local landmark for many residents, the house last known as Land's End was last lived in by Virginia Kraft Payson, wife of the late Charles Shipmen Payson, who sold the home in 2004 for $17.5 million and reported that she left the home in good repair. She was shocked to hear builder Burt Brodsky's claim that it cost him $1,642,500 a year, or "$4,500 a day," for insurance, taxes, and maintenance. It was a high number for a house that went from good condition to in ruins in seven years, according to Payson. (WD.)

**LA SELVA, 2011 AND KNOLE, 1996.**
Coming to the North Shore for the same reasons as the great estate builders, the entertainment industry has thought it a convenient and beautiful backdrop for nearly a century. Besides, where else could studios find a French château, a Georgian manor, Gothic castle, or Italian villa within one hour's drive from Manhattan? In television's *Pan Am* (2011), La Selva (above) stands in for a Roman café, and Knole's rotunda (right), seen in *The Associate* (1996), has over a dozen movies to its credit. Fictitious and true stories about Long Island, its houses, and residents became big Hollywood hits, including *Sabrina* (1954 and 1995). Ironically, the film version of *The Great Gatsby* (1974), the North Shore's most popular story, was actually filmed in Newport, Rhode Island; and the 2012 remake was shot in Australia. The Gold Coast is still a popular choice for residents and filmmakers; as long as its diverse landscape and great homes are preserved, films and stories will keep rolling far into the future. (Both, PJM.)

127

Visit us at
arcadiapublishing.com

CPSIA information can be obtained
at www.ICGtesting.com
Printed in the USA
BVOW09*0502301116
469265BV00015B/41/P